PEARSON LONG

CORNERSTONE

4

PEARSON English Learning System

Anna Uhl Chamot

Jim Cummins

Sharroky Hollie

PEARSON

Upper Saddle River, New Jersey • Boston, Massachusetts • Chandler, Arizona • Glenview, Illinois

Pearson Longman Cornerstone 4

PEARSON English Learning System

Staff credits: The people who made up the Longman Cornerstone team, representing editorial, production, design, manufacturing, and marketing, are John Ade, Rhea Banker, Virginia Bernard, Daniel Comstock, David Dickey, Gina DiLillo, Johnnie Farmer, Nancy Flaggman, Charles Green, Karen Kawaguchi, Ed Lamprich, Niki Lee, Jaime Leiber, Chris Leonowicz, Tara Maceyak, Linda Moser, Laurie Neaman, Leslie Patterson, Sherri Pemberton, Liza Pleva, Susan Saslow, Chris Siley, Loretta Steeves, Kim Steiner, and Lauren Weidenman.

Text design and composition: The Quarasan Group, Inc.
Illustration and photo credits appear on page 425, which constitute an extension of this copyright page.

Library of Congress Cataloging-in-Publication Data
Chamot, Anna Uhl.
    Longman Cornerstone / Anna Uhl Chamot, Jim Cummins, Sharroky Hollie.
    p. cm. — (Longman Cornerstone)
    Includes index.
    Contents: 1. Level 1. — 2. Level 2. — 3. Level 3. — 4. Level 4. — 5. Level 5.
    1. English language—Textbooks for foreign speakers. (1. English language—Textbooks for foreign speakers. 2. Readers.) I. Cummins, Jim. II. Hollie, Sharroky. III. Title.

ISBN-13: 978-0-328-77113-4
ISBN-10: 0-328-77113-9

Printed in the United States of America
12   17

Anna Uhl Chamot is a professor of secondary education and a faculty advisor for ESL in George Washington University's Department of Teacher Preparation. She has been a researcher and teacher trainer in content-based, second-language learning and language-learning strategies. She co-designed and has written extensively about the Cognitive Academic Language Learning Approach (CALLA) and spent seven years implementing the CALLA model in the Arlington Public Schools in Virginia.

Jim Cummins is the Canada Research Chair in the Department of Curriculum, Teaching, and Learning of the Ontario Institute for Studies in Education at the University of Toronto. His research focuses on literacy development in multilingual school contexts, as well as on the potential roles of technology in promoting language and literacy development. His recent publications include: *The International Handbook of English Language Teaching* (co-edited with Chris Davison) and *Literacy, Technology, and Diversity: Teaching for Success in Changing Times* (with Kristin Brown and Dennis Sayers).

Sharroky Hollie is an assistant professor in teacher education at California State University, Dominguez Hills. His expertise is in the field of professional development, African-American education, and second-language methodology. He is an urban literacy visiting professor at Webster University, St. Louis. Sharroky is the Executive Director of the Center for Culturally Responsive Teaching and Learning (CCRTL) and the co-founding director of the nationally-acclaimed Culture and Language Academy of Success (CLAS).

Rebecca Anselmo
Sunrise Acres Elementary School
Las Vegas, NV

Ana Applegate
Redlands School District
Redlands, CA

Terri Armstrong
Houston ISD
Houston, TX

Jacqueline Avritt
Riverside County Office of Ed.
Hemet, CA

Mitchell Bobrick
Palm Beach County School
West Palm Beach, FL

Victoria Brioso-Saldala
Broward County Schools
Fort Lauderdale, FL

Brenda Cabarga Schubert
Creekside Elementary School
Salinas, CA

Joshua Ezekiel
Bardin Elementary School
Salinas, CA

Veneshia Gonzalez
Seminole Elementary School
Okeechobee, FL

Carolyn Grigsby
San Francisco Unified School District
San Francisco, CA

Julie Grubbe
Plainfield Consolidated Schools
Chicago, IL

Yasmin Hernandez-Manno
Newark Public Schools
Newark, NJ

Janina Kusielewicz
Clifton Public Schools/Bilingual Ed.
& Basic Skills Instruction Dept.
Clifton, NJ

Mary Helen Lechuga
El Paso ISD
El Paso, TX

Gayle P. Malloy
Randolph School District
Randolph, MA

Randy Payne
Patterson/Taft Elementaries
Mesa, AZ

Marcie L. Schnegelberger
Alisal Union SD
Salinas, CA

Lorraine Smith
Collier County Schools
Naples, FL

Shawna Stoltenborg
Glendale Elementary School
Glen Burnie, MD

Denise Tiffany
West High School
Iowa City, IO

Dear Student,

Welcome to Longman Cornerstone!

We wrote *Longman Cornerstone* to help you succeed in all your school studies. This program will help you learn the English language you need to study language arts, social studies, math, and science. You will learn how to speak to family members, classmates, and teachers in English.

Cornerstone includes a mix of many subjects. Each unit has four different readings that include some fiction (made-up) and nonfiction (true) articles, stories, songs, and poems. The readings will give you some of the tools you need to do well in all your subjects in school.

As you use this program, you will build on what you already know and learn new words, new information and facts, and take part in creative activities. The activities will help you improve your English skills.

Learning a language takes time, but just like learning to skateboard or learning to swim, it is fun!

We hope you enjoy *Longman Cornerstone* as much as we enjoyed writing it for you!

Good luck!

Anna Uhl Chamot
Jim Cummins
Sharroky Hollie

Animals, People, and Caring

THE BIG Q QUESTION

Powerful Forces of Nature

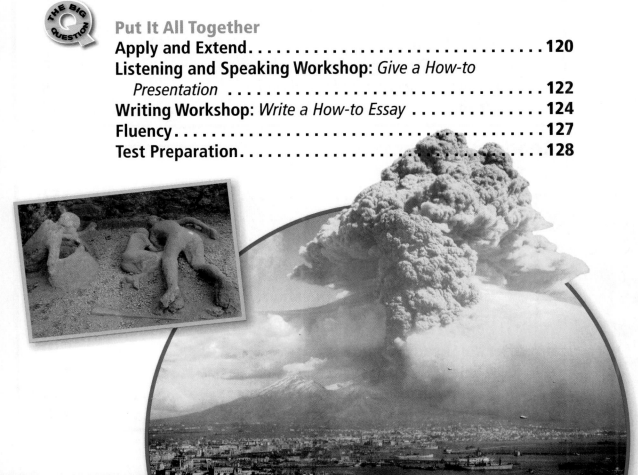

Reading 3: Literature/Short Story

THE BIG Q QUESTION

Telling Tales

Contents

Problem Solvers

Reading 3: Informational Text/Social Studies

    More About the Big Question
    Reading Strategy: *Identify Cause and Effect*

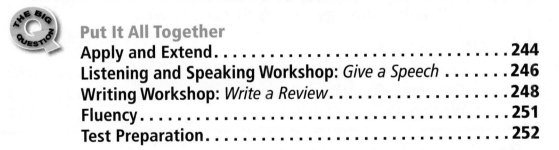

Put It All Together

Where We Live

Reading 3: Informational Text/Biography

 More About the Big Question
 Reading Strategy: *Visualize*

Put It All Together

Links to Our Past

Reading 3: Informational Text/Social Studies

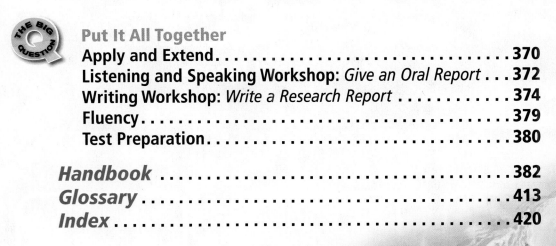

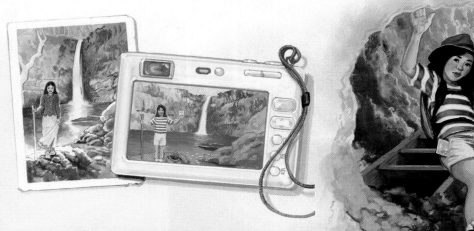

Animals, People, and Caring

Animals are fun to be around. Some keep us company. Other animals help us. It is important to take care of our animal friends.

Reading

1 | Science

Taking Care of the Young

2 | Fable

The Star Llama

3 | Social Studies

Mustangs

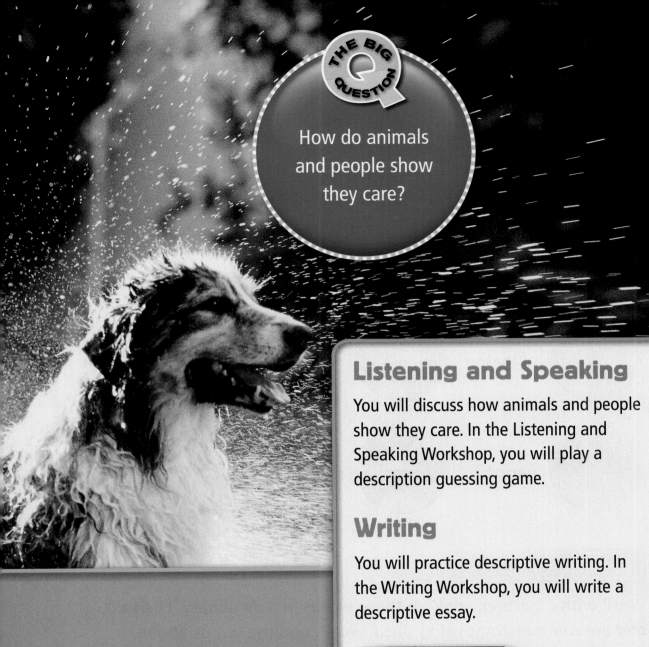

THE BIG QUESTION

How do animals and people show they care?

Listening and Speaking

You will discuss how animals and people show they care. In the Listening and Speaking Workshop, you will play a description guessing game.

Writing

You will practice descriptive writing. In the Writing Workshop, you will write a descriptive essay.

Quick Write

Why do you think people like animals? Write your answer in your notebook.

DVD **VIEW AND RESPOND**
Talk about the poster for this unit. Then watch and listen to the video and answer the questions at LongmanCornerstone.com.

What do you know about animals?

Words to Know

Listen and repeat. Use these words to talk about animals.

 alligator

 raccoon

 elephant

 parrot

 skunk

 giraffe

Practice

Work with a partner. Look up these words in a dictionary. Then ask and answer questions using these words and the words above.

a bird	a mammal	a reptile

Example: A: What kind of animal is an _alligator_?

B: An _alligator_ is _a_ reptile.

Write

Read the question. Write your response in your notebook.

What other birds, mammals, and reptiles do you know?

Make Connections

Copy the sentences below into your notebook. Complete the sentences with the following words.

a swamp

a rain forest

the woodlands

the grasslands

1. _____ is often warm and rainy. Parrots and monkeys live here.

2. There are plenty of trees in _____. Raccoons and skunks are often found here.

3. _____ do not have a lot of trees, but they do have plenty of grass. Elephants and zebras live here.

4. _____ is a wetland. There is a lot of water, and alligators and frogs live here.

What about you?

Talk with a partner. Talk about your favorite wild animals. Where do they live?

Kids' Stories from around the World 🎵 Audio

Morocco

Gre

Hassan

Camels are very important in Morocco. They help us cross the desert. A group of camels is called a caravan. Camels can live for days without water.

Cassandra

I live on Santorini. It is an island in Greece. The streets are very steep. Our donkeys carry people and packages. I brush my donkey to keep him clean.

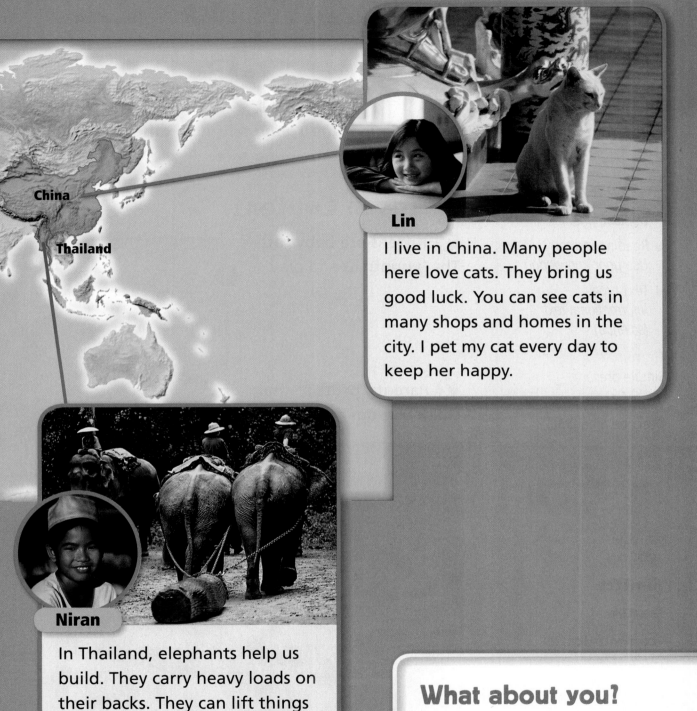

Lin

I live in China. Many people here love cats. They bring us good luck. You can see cats in many shops and homes in the city. I pet my cat every day to keep her happy.

Niran

In Thailand, elephants help us build. They carry heavy loads on their backs. They can lift things with their strong trunks. They can also drag heavy loads. I feed my elephants grass and leaves. This food keeps them strong and healthy.

What about you?

1. Which animal do you think helps people the most? Why?

2. Do you know a story about animals? Share your story.

Prepare to Read

What You Will Learn

Reading
- Vocabulary building: *Context, phonics*
- Reading strategy: *Use prior knowledge*
- Text type: *Informational text (science)*

Grammar
Simple present

Writing
Describe an animal

These words will help you understand the reading.

Key Words

young

protect

secure

communicates

Key Words

Taking Care of the Young tells how different animals keep their young safe.

Words in Context

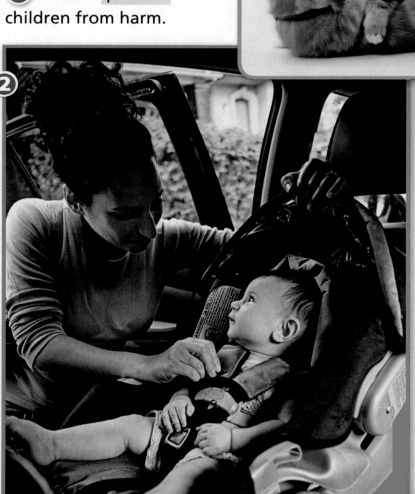

1 Kittens are baby cats. The young like to play.

2 Parents protect their children from harm.

3 Animals try to keep their young secure.

4 A dog communicates by barking and by wagging its tail.

Practice

Make flashcards to help you memorize the words.
- Write a key word on the front.
- On the back, write the meaning.

Make Connections

Sometimes, animals need our help. Have you ever heard about an animal that needed help? Use some of the key words as you speak.

3

These words will help you talk about the reading.

Academic Words

challenge
something that is hard to do

goal
something you want to achieve

involve
include, or be part of

Academic Words

Words in Context Audio

A penguin father has the **challenge** of keeping the chicks warm in freezing temperatures.

Emily's **goal** was to run five miles.

The science fair will **involve** everyone in the class.

Practice

Write the sentences in your notebook. Choose an academic word to complete each sentence.

1. The math test was a real ___.

2. The care of a community garden can ___ many people.

3. The ___ of the food drive is to collect food for hungry people.

Apply

Write the answers in your notebook. Use the academic words. Then ask and answer with a partner.

1. What school subjects **involve** using the Internet?

2. What **goals** do you have for this school year?

3. Will reaching those goals be a **challenge**?

Phonics

Short Vowels

Each word in the chart has one vowel. Listen.
Then read each word aloud.

a	e	i	o	u
can	get	big	fox	cub
bag	den	his	not	pup

Rule

A word is likely to have a short vowel sound when:

- it has a single vowel.
- the vowel has a single consonant before and after it.

c a n   g e t   p u p

C V C   C V C   C V C

Practice

Work with a partner. Copy the chart.

- Find the CVC word or words in each sentence.
- List each CVC word in the correct column.
- Read each word aloud.

   1. I fed my cat today.

   2. Horses like to rub noses.

   3. A chicken can be a family pet.

   4. A group of whales is a pod.

   5. A pig can run in a pen.

Short Vowel Sound				
a	e	i	o	u

5

INFORMATIONAL TEXT

Science

More About THE BIG QUESTION

Why is it important for animals to take care of their young?

 Listen to the Audio.
Listen for the general meaning. Use the pictures to help you understand the selection.

Reading Strategy

Use Prior Knowledge

Before you read, ask yourself these questions:

- What do I already know about animals taking care of their young?

- What do I want to find out about animals taking care of their young?

- Copy the chart on page 23. Fill in the first two columns.

Listen as your teacher models the reading strategy.

Taking Care of the Young

Adult penguins watch their chicks.

Penguins

Human babies need adults to protect them. Animal babies need parents, too.

Both male and **female** emperor penguins take care of their babies. The mother lays an egg. Then the father keeps the egg warm while the mother looks for food.

Emperor penguin chicks stay close to their parents at all times. One parent will stay and watch the chicks. The other will go find food. Then he or she will bring the food back for the babies to eat. The parents work together to keep their babies safe.

_____

human person

female girl or woman

Reading Skill
The yellow highlighted word **protect** is a key word.

Before You Go On The penguin parents work together toward what **goal**?

Swans

Swans also take care of their young. One parent stays with the babies at all times. This keeps them safe and secure. The babies cannot fly for many months after they are born. It is hard for them to escape **danger** when they cannot fly.

The adult swans work hard to keep other animals away from their babies. They also teach their babies how to take care of themselves. Soon, they will be old enough to fly. Then they will leave their parents.

---

danger   something that can cause harm

This mother swan watches her babies.

Raccoons

Raccoon babies are very small when they are born. They cannot stand or open their eyes. Only female raccoons take care of the babies. A mother might have four babies to take care of alone. She must leave them in the **den** when she looks for food. In the den, the raccoon babies are safe from danger.

The mother raccoon worries that other animals might find her den. So after a few months, the family moves. By then, the babies can walk and climb. Their mother has taught them to take care of themselves.

---

den   home for animals that is hidden

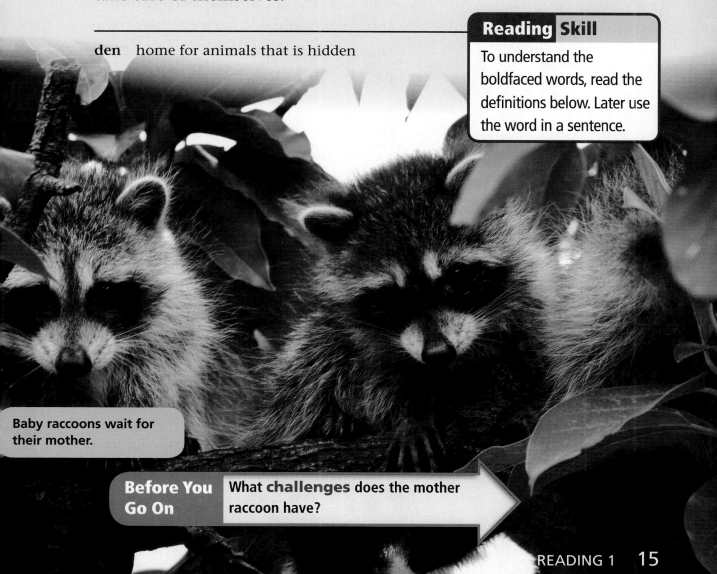

Baby raccoons wait for their mother.

Before You Go On   What **challenges** does the mother raccoon have?

Wallabies

Mother wallabies have an unusual way to protect their babies. They carry their babies in a **pouch**. A baby wallaby, called a joey, has no fur when it is born. The baby climbs into its mother's pouch to stay warm. The wallaby's pouch also **guards** the joey from danger.

When a joey gets older, it will sometimes leave its mother's pouch. But mother wallabies still try to keep their babies safe. If a mother wallaby senses trouble, she communicates with her baby. She stomps on the ground. This tells her joey to return to her pouch.

---

pouch   pocket used to carry things

guards   protects or keeps safe

This baby wallaby is protected in its mother's pouch.

Reading Skill

Read the caption that goes with each picture. This will help you to understand both the words and the pictures.

Clown Fish

All animal parents have to be careful. Even fish parents watch for danger in the water. Clown fish fathers guard their eggs carefully to keep them safe. They keep other fish away from their eggs. They also keep the eggs clean.

After the eggs **hatch**, the babies will swim away from their parents. Now they are on their own. Soon, they will find a place to live. Later, they will become parents themselves. They will have their own eggs to protect.

---

hatch   come out of an egg

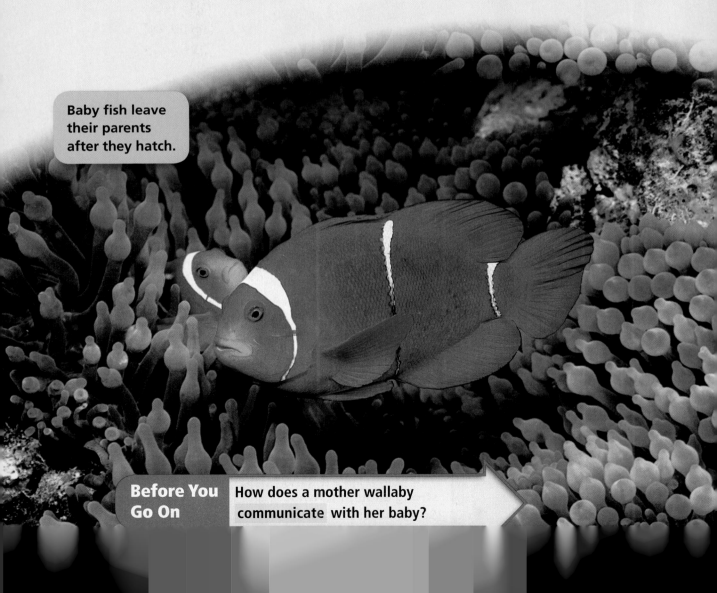

Baby fish leave their parents after they hatch.

Before You Go On   How does a mother wallaby communicate with her baby?

People

Human mothers and fathers take care of their young. They must watch their children carefully. When it is cold, they put hats and sweaters on their children to keep them warm. Sometimes, they carry their young in their arms or on their shoulders.

Human children and animal babies keep their parents busy! How are these animals just like people?

Young lion cubs are not strong enough to walk. So a mother lion carries her cub with her mouth.

A penguin keeps its chick warm in the cold.

A bear cub likes to play and run. Its mother needs to watch it carefully.

WB
6–8

Reading Strategy

Use Prior Knowlege

- How did your knowledge of animals and people help you understand the reading?
- What have you learned about taking care of the young?
- What else would you like to learn?
- Ask your teacher or classmates if you don't understand.

Think It Over

1. **Recall** Where does the mother wallaby carry her babies?

2. **Comprehend** What is **involved** with caring for the clown fish eggs?

3. **Analyze** How do human children keep their parents busy? Explain.

Animals and Their Young

▲ Goose and goslings
This mother goose has two goslings.

▲ Lion and cub
A mother lion keeps her cub clean.

◀ Horse and foal
A horse runs with her new foal.

▲ Eagle and chick

An eagle feeds its chick. They live in a nest high in a tree.

▲ Hyena and pups

A hyena looks a little like a dog. Its babies are called pups.

▲ Deer and fawn

A young deer is called a fawn. It has spots to help it hide in the woods.

▲ Cow and calf

The young calf stands in a field with two cows.

Activity to Do

These two pages tell you more about adult animals and their babies.

- Choose an animal.
- Research the animal online or in the library.
- Tell about the animal's babies using pictures and words.

Learning Strategies

Reread for Details

You can reread a selection to find information.

Practice

Tell if each statement below is TRUE or FALSE. Tell the page number you found the answer on.

1. Only the male emperor penguin takes care of penguin chicks.
2. Baby swans leave their parents when they can fly.
3. Only female raccoons take care of baby raccoons.
4. The father clown fish shows the babies how to swim.

Use a KWL Chart

A KWL Chart helps you remember three kinds of information:

1. What you **Know** about a topic before reading

2. What you **Want** to learn about the topic

3. What you **Learned** about the topic

Before reading, you completed the first two columns.
Now complete the third column: What I Learned.

- Begin by adding new details you remember.
- Then look back in the selection to recall other details.

Topic: Taking Care of the Young		
What I Know	What I Want to Learn	What I Learned

9

1. What is something that you still want to learn about how animals care for their young?

2. Where might you look to find this information?

Explain how animals take care of their young to a partner. Use some of the key words.

Extension

Utilize Form a small group and choose a favorite animal. Write a skit about that animal and its babies. Be sure to listen carefully to your classmates and work together. Use informal language in your skit. You can speak using simple sentences and slang.

Reading 1

Grammar

Simple Present

Use the **simple present tense** for things that happen regularly or are generally true. With singular subjects (*he, she, it*), add *-s* to the plain form of the verb. With *I* and plural subjects (*they, we*) use the plain form of the verb.

Subject	Simple Present	
She	communicates	with her baby.
They	communicate	with their babies.

Make the **negative** form of regular verbs with *does not, do not*, or a contraction and the plain form of the verb.

Singular Negative
She **doesn't guard** the egg. ⟶ **Plural Negative**
They **don't stay** with their parents.

Make sure **the verb *be*** agrees with the subject.

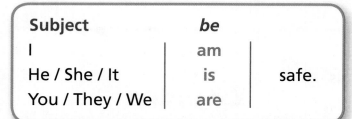

Subject	*be*	
I	am	
He / She / It	is	safe.
You / They / We	are	

I am not = **I'm not**
are not = **aren't**
is not = **isn't**

Make the **negative** form of *be* verbs with *not* or use a contraction.

Singular Negative
It **isn't** in danger. ⟶ **Plural Negative**
The babies **aren't** on their own.

To make questions with regular verbs, use *does* or *do*. Be sure to use the correct form of *be* verbs.

Does he **guard** the egg? **Are** they **safe?**

Practice

Complete each sentence with the correct
form of the verb. Write the sentences.

Example: The parent <u>carries</u> her young . (carry)

1. It _____ safe and secure . (be)

2. They _____ on their own. (be)

3. We _____ with our parents. (communicate)

4. She _____ the joey from danger. (protect)

5. They _____ for food. (look)

Apply

Work with a partner. Ask and answer the questions about
Taking Care of the Young. If you need to, look back at
the reading.

Example: A: Why do animal babies need parents?

B: They need parents to protect them.

- Why do animal babies need parents?
- What does a mother penguin look for?
- Why does one swan stay with the babies?
- Where are baby raccoons safe from danger?
- What does a mother wallaby carry in her pouch?
- Why does a mother wallaby stomp on the ground?
- Does a clown fish mother guard the eggs?

10

**Grammar
Check ✓**

What are the
contractions for *do
not* and *does not*?

Writing

Ongoing Writing Skills Practice

Describe an Animal

A description is a picture made up of words. When you describe something, you include details that tell how it looks and acts. You can also describe how it sounds, smells, tastes, and feels to help your reader experience it.

Writing Prompt

Write a description of an animal. The animal can be real or from your imagination. Be sure to use present tense verbs correctly, including forms of *be* and regular verbs.

❶ Prewrite

Choose an animal to write about. Think about the words you will use to describe the animal. Write the name of the animal in the center of a word web. On the spokes, write words that describe the animal.

A student named Jill listed her ideas in this word web:

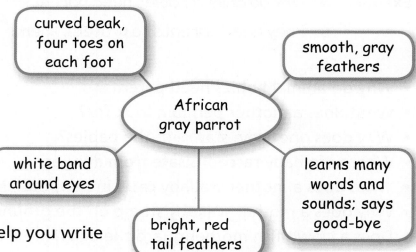

- curved beak, four toes on each foot
- smooth, gray feathers
- African gray parrot
- white band around eyes
- learns many words and sounds; says good-bye
- bright, red tail feathers

❷ Draft

Use your word web to help you write a first draft.

- Keep in mind your purpose for writing—to describe.
- Use words that describe how the animal looks, acts, sounds, and feels.

❸ Revise

Read over your draft. Look for places where the writing needs improvement. Use the Writing Checklist to help you identify problems. Then revise your draft.

❹ Edit

Check your work for errors. Trade papers with a partner to get feedback. Use the Peer Review Checklist on page 402. Edit your final draft in response to feedback from your partner and your teacher.

❺ Publish

Prepare a clean copy of your final draft. Share your paragraph with the class. Save your work. You'll need to refer to it in the Writing Workshop at the end of the unit.

Here is Jill's paragraph:

Writing Checklist

Ideas

✓ I told how the animal looks, acts, and sounds.

Sentence Fluency

✓ I used sentences of different lengths and types.

Conventions

✓ My nouns, pronouns, and verbs agree.

Jill Lee

I am at the children's zoo with my class. The zookeeper shows us an African gray parrot. The bird is beautiful. It has a powerful curved beak. On each foot it has four toes with long claws. Its feathers are smooth and gray. There is a white band around the bird's eyes. Its eyes look smart. The parrot's bright red tail feathers gleam in the sunlight. This amazing bird learns many words and other sounds. When our class leaves, the parrot says good-bye.

WB
11–12

Prepare to Read

What You Will Learn

Reading

- Vocabulary building: *Context, word study*
- Reading strategy: *Identify fantasy and reality*
- Text Type: *Literature (fable)*

Grammar

Simple past: *be* verbs

Writing

Describe yourself

These words will help you understand the reading.

Key Words

- shimmer
- frisky
- glowed
- warm
- breath
- companion

Key Words

The Star Llama is about a boy and his llama.

Words in Context

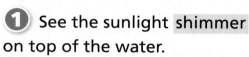

1 See the sunlight shimmer on top of the water.

2 Many young animals are frisky. Just like human children, they love to play.

3 The fireflies glowed in the jar.

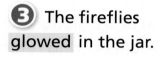

4 Some babies get cold easily. Their mothers help keep them warm.

5 You can see an animal's breath when it is cold outside.

6 A pet can be a good companion. This puppy will keep these people company on a picnic.

Create a vocabulary notebook.

- Divide your page into three columns: the new words, their definitions, and drawings of the words when possible.

- Test yourself by covering one of the columns.

Make Connections

In the next story, a boy is helped by a special friend. Narrate a story about how a friend helped you. How did it make you feel?

13

These words will help you talk about the reading.

Academic Words

bond
special relationship or connection

encounter
a meeting

occur
to happen or take place

Academic Words

Words in Context

Children and dogs often form strong **bonds**.

An **encounter** between a dog and a cat can be very noisy.

When it rains for a long time, floods can **occur**.

Write the sentences in your notebook. Choose an academic word to complete each sentence.

1. When storms _____, the ball games stop.

2. The girls saw their teacher at the movies. The _____ surprised them all.

3. Students can form a _____ of friendship by playing on the same team.

Apply

Write the answers in your notebook. Use the academic words. Then ask and answer with a partner.

1. With what friend do you have a strong **bond**?

2. In a first **encounter** with a new teacher, many students are shy. Are you?

3. What are some activities that **occur** in your school?

Word Study

Endings: *-s, -es, -ed*

A **verb** names an action. The ending of a verb tells when the action happened. Listen. Then read each sentence aloud.

> Today the boy **walks** many miles without his llama.
>
> Now the boy **searches** for the star llama.
>
> Yesterday, the boy **walked** many miles.

Reading Skill

Looking for patterns in English will make you a better reader.

Rule

Look for this pattern in English: The endings *-s* and *-es* tell what the boy does now. The ending *-ed* tells what the boy did in the past.

walk**s** = walk + *s*   search**es** = search + *es*
walk**ed** = walk + *ed*

Practice

Work with a partner. Take turns reading the sentences aloud.

- Charlie the llama plays in a field.
- His hair reaches down to the ground.
- Charlie wanted to visit new places.
- He runs around the yard.

1. List each verb in the correct column.
2. Look in the story. Find three words ending in *-ed*.

Verbs with Endings		
-s	-es	-ed

15

LITERATURE
Fable

More About

In what ways can animals help the people who care for them?

 Listen to the Audio.
Listen for the general meaning. Use the pictures to help you understand the selection.

Reading Strategy

Identify Fantasy and Reality

Many stories describe events that can happen in real life. But sometimes, stories describe things that could never happen in reality.

- Read the title.
- Look at the pictures.
- Think about parts of the story that could be real.
- Think about parts of the story that must be fantasy.

Listen as your teacher models the reading strategy.

The Star Llama

by Jan Mike
illustrated by Theresa Smith

Once there was a young **Inca** boy. He had no family except for an old **llama**. Each day, the boy and his companion walked many miles, looking for a home. Each night, they curled up together and slept. But one starry evening, the old llama died.

Inca person from an ancient culture in the Andes mountains in South America

llama South American animal with thick hair like wool and a long neck

Before You Go On Could the event in this picture really **occur**?

The boy buried his friend next to an icy **stream**. Then he sat under a tree and cried. What would he do, he thought. He had no family and no home.

The boy cried for a very long time. But there was no one to comfort him. There were only the stars in the sky.

---

stream   flow of water that moves across the land and is narrower than a river

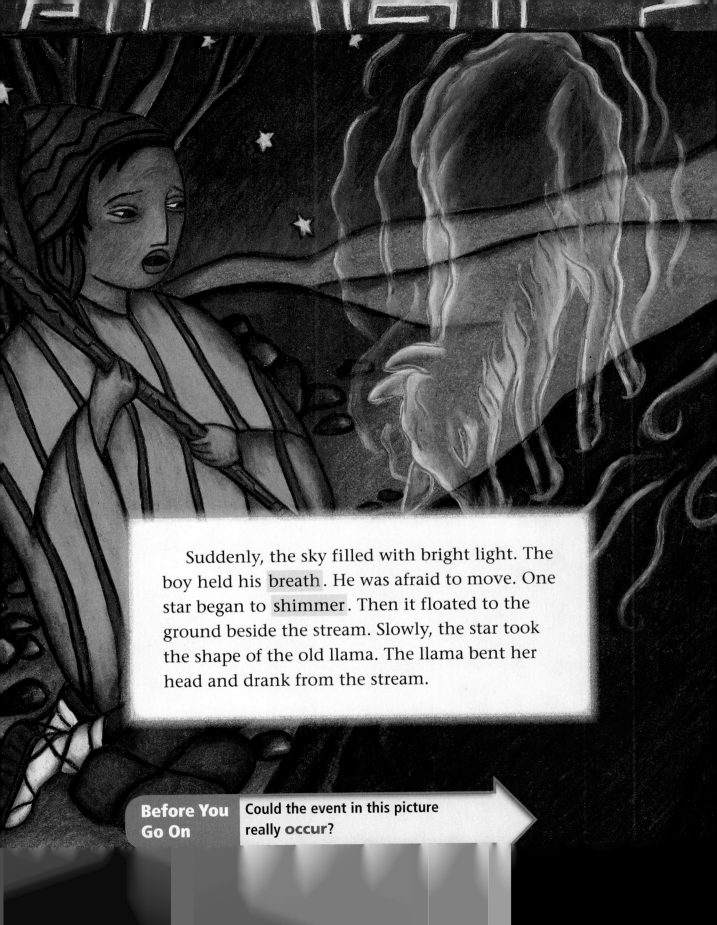

Suddenly, the sky filled with bright light. The boy held his breath . He was afraid to move. One star began to shimmer . Then it floated to the ground beside the stream. Slowly, the star took the shape of the old llama. The llama bent her head and drank from the stream.

Before You Go On

Could the event in this picture really **occur**?

The star llama drank for a very long time. Then she looked at the sad Inca boy and smiled. When she jumped back into the sky, bits of llama wool fell. The boy felt the silver wool. It was soft and warm.

As the sun began to rise, the boy **gathered** the llama wool. It glowed in his hands like starlight. He carried the wool to the city and sold it. With the money, he bought a house and two frisky young llamas. He never forgot the star llama. And he was never lonely again.

---

gathered collected

W B

16–18

Reading Strategy

Identify Fantasy and Reality

- Which parts of the story could be real?
- Which parts are fantasy?
- Did telling fantasy from reality help you understand the story? How?

Think It Over

1. **Recall** Where does this story take place?

2. **Comprehend** Describe the **bond** between the boy and the old llama.

3. **Analyze** How did the **encounter** with the star llama change the boy's life?

Learning Strategies

Fantasy and Reality

Some stories are **fantasy,** or make-believe. The characters or the settings are not real. The events could never happen.

Other stories are real. They are based on **reality,** or the real world. The events could happen. Some stories have both fantasy and reality in them.

Practice

Read each sentence. Ask yourself, *Could this really happen?*

- If the answer is *yes*, write R for reality.
- If the answer is *no*, write F for fantasy.

1. A boy and a llama walk many miles in the Andes Mountains.

2. The boy goes to sleep next to his llama.

3. The boy sits under a tree and cries.

4. A star takes the shape of a llama.

5. The star llama drinks from the stream.

Use a T-Chart

A T-chart helps readers understand a story that has both fantasy and reality. It also helps readers look more closely at the characters, setting, or plot of a story.

Copy the chart.

- Write the sentences from the previous page in the correct column.
- Then reread the story.
- Find another sentence for the Fantasy column and another sentence for the Reality column.

Fantasy	Reality
	A boy and a llama walk many miles in the Andes Mountains.

Compare your chart with a partner's. Discuss what makes *The Star Llama* a fantasy story and not realistic fiction.

Using the pictures in the reading, retell the story to a partner.

19

Grammar

Simple Past: *be* verbs

Use the **simple past tense** to talk about something that occurred or was true in the past. When you use the **simple past** of *be*, make sure it agrees with the subject.

Subject	Past Tense: *be*	
I / He / She / It	was	
You / We / They →	were	warm .

Make the **past negative** form of *be* with *not* or a **contraction**.

Affirmative Past	Negative Past
He was frisky . →	He wasn't frisky.
They were young.	They weren't young.

was not = **wasn't**
were not = **weren't**

For **Yes-No questions** and **Wh-questions**, make sure the verb agrees with the subject. If there is no subject, use *was*.

Yes-No Questions
  Was he lonely?
  Were they companions ?
Wh-Question with subject (they)
  Where were they?
Wh-Question without subject
  What was in the sky?

Practice

Change each simple present *be* verb to
the past tense. Write the sentences.

Example: The boy and his dog are companions.

The boy and his dog were companions.

1. The boy is not alone.

2. There is a special **bond** between them.

3. The **encounter** with the bear is a fantasy.

4. The old cat isn't frisky.

5. They aren't lonely at their grandmother's house.

Apply

Work with a partner. Ask and answer the questions about
what you were like when you were younger.

Example: A: What were you like when you were six?

B: When I was six, I was shy.

- What were you like when you were six?
- What was your favorite animal?
- What were your favorite foods?
- What was your favorite toy?
- What were you afraid of?
- Who was your best friend?
- What were your favorite songs?

20

Grammar Check ✓

Name the past
negative contractions
for the verb *be*.

Writing

Describe Yourself

Ongoing Writing Skills Practice

How would you describe yourself as a younger person? Answer these questions: *What did you look like? How did you act? What did you like and dislike?* Writers use the pronouns *I, me,* and *my* when they write about themselves.

Writing Prompt

Write a paragraph that describes a photograph of yourself when you were younger. Be sure to use the past tense of *be* verbs correctly.

❶ Prewrite

Find a photograph of yourself that was taken when you were younger. Then write a short description of how you look in the photograph. List your ideas in a word web.

A student named Ricky listed his ideas in this word web:

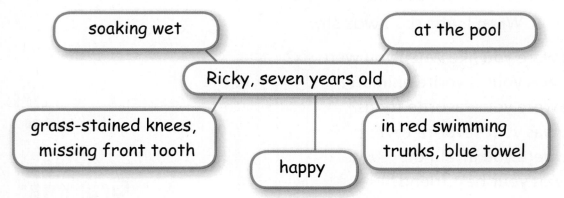

❷ Draft

Use your word web to help you write a first draft.

- Keep in mind your purpose—to describe.
- Use words to show how you acted, looked, thought, and felt.

❸ Revise

Read your draft. Look for places where the writing is uninteresting or unclear. Use the Writing Checklist to help you identify problems. Then revise your draft.

❹ Edit

Check your work for errors. Trade papers with a partner to get feedback. Use the Peer Review Checklist on page 402. Edit your final draft in response to feedback from your partner and your teacher.

❺ Publish

Prepare a clean copy of your final draft. Share your paragraph with the class. Save your work. You'll need to refer to it in the Writing Workshop at the end of the unit.

Here is Ricky's paragraph:

Writing Checklist

Ideas

✓ I described how I looked and felt.

Conventions

✓ I used the past tense of *be* verbs correctly.

✓ My nouns, pronouns, and verbs agree.

Ricky Torres

When I was seven years old, I was at the swimming pool almost every day. I was soaking wet. My swimming trunks were red, and my towel was blue with yellow and green stripes. My knees were grass-stained and my front tooth was missing. I remember that I was very happy that day. It was a great day! To me, the pool was the best place in the world!

What You Will Learn

Reading
- Vocabulary building: *Context, phonics*
- Reading strategy: *Preview*
- Text type: *Informational text (social studies)*

Grammar
Simple past: regular verbs

Writing
Describe a place you visit

These words will help you understand the reading.

Key Words

feral

mustangs

captured

breeders

banned

Key Words

Mustangs is about wild horses that roam the American West.

Words in Context

1 A feral animal is an animal that used to be tame but now lives in the wild. Some mustangs are feral horses.

2 The fish was captured in the net.

3 Dog breeders raise puppies to sell to other people.

4 The United States has banned, or passed laws against, any mistreatment of animals.

Practice

Add a page to your vocabulary notebook.

- Divide your page into three columns: the new words, their definitions, and drawings of the words when possible.
- Test yourself by covering one of the columns.

Make Connections

Have you ever seen a feral animal? What kind of feral animal was it? Where did you see it?

23

These words will help you talk about the reading.

Academic Words

establish
get something started, such as a company, system, or situation

recover
get back to a healthy condition

strategy
plan used to reach a goal

Academic Words

Words in Context

People wanted to **establish** farms in the West so they would have a lot of land.

The doctor said the patient will fully **recover** from the illness.

Previewing is a **strategy** you can use to understand a reading selection.

Practice

Write the sentences in your notebook. Choose an academic word to complete each sentence.

1. The team had a new _____ so they won the game.

2. I was sick for two days, but on the third day I began to _____.

3. Tyrone is going to _____ a new club at school that helps animals.

Apply

Write the answers in your notebook. Use the academic words. Then ask and answer with a partner.

1. How might you **establish** a new club at school?

2. How do **recover** from an illness?

3. What **strategy** could you use to prepare for a difficult exam?

24

Phonics

Long Vowels with Silent *e*

The words in the chart follow the CVCe pattern. Listen to your teacher say each word. Then sound out the words in the box.

a_e	i_e	o_e	u_e
cane	like	note	cube
made	time	home	cute
save	life	hope	mule

Rule

When the first vowel in a one-syllable word is followed by both a consonant and an *e*, the vowel is usually long. The final *e* is silent.

c a n e	l i k e	c u b e
C V C e	C V C e	C V C e

Work with a partner. Take turns.

1. Read the CVC words aloud.

2. Add an e to each word to write a CVCe word.

3. Read the CVCe words aloud.

4. Write a sentence using the new words.

CVC Words	CVCe Words
bit	
cod	
fad	
fin	

More About

THE BIG QUESTION

How do people help and care for wild animals?

Audio **Listen to the Audio.**
Listen for the general meaning. Use the pictures to help you understand the selection.

Reading Strategy

Preview

Before you read, preview the selection. Previewing helps you start thinking about what you will read. To preview, follow these steps:

- Read the title.
- Study the photographs and the captions.
- Predict what this section will be about.

Listen as your teacher models the reading strategy.

Mustangs

When Spanish explorers came to America, they brought horses. The first horses came to the western United States in the 1500s. As the explorers traveled through the Southwest, some horses escaped. They lived in herds in the wild. By the 1800s, about two million horses **roamed** the American West.

People called these horses mustangs, from the Spanish word *mestengo*. *Mestengo* means "stray animal." We often call mustangs "wild." But scientists call them "feral." A feral animal is an animal that used to be tame but now lives in the wild.

Mustangs lived in harsh country. They became strong and **rugged**. They developed hard hooves.

---

roamed   wandered
rugged   tough

Some Native Americans captured and trained mustangs. Native Americans became skilled at riding horses. Hunting and traveling became easier on horseback. Horses helped Native Americans carry their **possessions** when they moved.

Cowboys also captured and trained mustangs. Mustangs could travel long distances. They were quick and **nimble** when working with cattle. Many cowboys rode mustangs to round up or gather the cattle that roamed across the American West.

Horse breeders saw the value in mustangs. They used mustangs to develop new American breeds. These breeds included the Quarter Horse, Morgan, and Tennessee Walker. The Nez Perce tribe bred mustangs to develop the Appaloosa.

---

possessions   things owned by a person or people

nimble   able to move easily and skillfully

Two million mustangs once roamed free in the American West.

Before You Go On   How were the first herds of wild horses **established** in the Southwest?

W B

More people began settling the West. They wanted land to raise cattle and other **livestock**. They sometimes killed mustangs to make room for their ranches. They sometimes rounded them up, using planes and trucks. One million mustangs were captured for soldiers to ride in World War I.

Velma Bronn Johnston was a ranch owner in Nevada. In 1950, she saw the bad things people were doing to the mustangs. She wanted to save them. She began speaking to ranchers, business people, and government officials. She became known as Wild Horse Annie.

---

livestock   animals kept on a ranch or farm

It is estimated that there are only about 20,000 wild horses in the United States today.

Because of Annie, people all over the United States wrote letters to **Congress**. Many letters came from school children. In 1971, Congress passed the Wild Free-Roaming Horses and Burros Act. Every member of Congress voted for the act. It protected wild horses and **burros** on public lands. It banned people from hurting, killing, or capturing the animals.

Today, nearly 37,000 mustangs and burros roam on public land. Ranchers pay to use some public land to raise livestock. But now companies use some of that land to drill for oil. Many people worry that mustangs are being pushed aside. They are still working to keep mustangs safe.

Many burros escaped from miners and ranchers and lived in the wild. Wild burros are also protected by the Wild Free-Roaming Horses and Burros Act.

Congress   part of the United States government that makes laws

burros   small donkeys

26–28

Reading Strategy

Preview

- How did previewing the title help you prepare for reading?

- What did previewing the photos and their captions tell you about the selection?

- Did previewing help you when you read? How?

Think It Over

1. **Recall**   Who brought the first horses to America?

2. **Comprehend**   What was Wild Horse Annie's **strategy** for saving the mustangs?

3. **Analyze**   How might the Wild Free-Roaming Horses and Burros Act help mustangs **recover** after they were hunted and treated badly for so many years?

Learning Strategies

Preview

Before you read the selection, you previewed it. When readers preview a story, they look at:

- titles
- subtitles
- photos or illustrations
- captions

Previewing helps readers understand a story. It tells you a little about the topic. Then you have some information about the topic before you start reading.

Horseback riding is a favorite activity for many children who live in the western United States.

Answer the following questions.

1. When you previewed this selection, what did the pictures and captions tell you?

2. Turn to page 78. Preview the text. What do you think it will be about?

3. Now turn to pages 94–95. Preview the text. What will this text be about?

Use a Details Chart

You can use a Details Chart to collect specific information from a text.

 G.O. 141

Copy this Details Chart.
- In the first box, write who captured the wild mustangs.
- Then add details about why the mustangs were captured.

Who Captured Mustangs		Detail 1	Detail 2	Detail 3
Cowboys	→	captured and trained them	rode to round up cattle	Mustangs could travel long distances.
	→			
	→			
	→			

1. How does the Details Chart help you find details?

2. Check your chart. Why was the Wild Free-Roaming Horses and Burros Act needed to save the mustangs?

29

Retell the selection to a partner using the photographs. Be sure to use the key words.

Extension

Utilize Talk with your partner about things that you are good at. How could you use those skills to help or care for animals? Present your ideas to the class using visuals.

Grammar

Simple Past: Regular Verbs

Use the **simple past tense** for actions that have already happened.
You can make the **simple past** of most **regular verbs** by adding -ed.

Present	Past
They **work** in the class. ⟶	They **worked** in the class.

To change some verbs to the simple past look at the endings.

Add -d to verbs ending in -e.	move ⟶	moved
For verbs ending in a consonant and -y, change the y to i and add -ed.	try ⟶	tried
For verbs ending in a vowel and -y, add -ed.	stay ⟶	stayed
For verbs with a stressed CVC ending, double the consonant and add -ed.	oc**cur** ⟶	occurred

Make the **past negative** form of regular verbs with
did not (or *didn't*) and the plain form of the verb.

did not = **didn't**

Affirmative Past	Negative Past
They **lived** in the wild. ⟶	They **didn't live** with people.

Make *Yes-No questions* and *Wh-questions* with *did* and the plain form of the verb when there is a subject. When there is no subject in a *Wh-*question, just use the past form of the verb.

Did they **work** on farms?
Where **did** they **find** help?
Who **called** them wild?

Change each regular verb to the simple past.
Write the sentences.

Example: They permit the horses to graze.

They permitted the horses to graze.

1. I stay after school.

2. The students name all of the horses.

3. We play soccer after school every day.

4. I prefer to do it myself.

5. The students study an hour a day.

Apply

Work with a partner. Use the regular verbs below to make
statements about things you do and things you've done
recently.

Example: A: I study math every night.

B: I studied last weekend.

- study
- like
- carry
- start
- learn

- clean
- save
- listen
- watch
- admit

WB
30

Grammar Check ✓

How do you form the
negative past of a
regular verb?

Writing

Ongoing Writing Skills Practice

Describe a Place You Visit

Writers often describe places they have visited. Their descriptions create exciting word pictures so other people can imagine these places. These descriptions answer the questions: How does the place look and smell? What do I think or how do I feel about the place?

Writing Prompt

Write a paragraph that describes a place you have visited. Be sure to use past tense regular verbs correctly.

❶ Prewrite G.O. 153

Choose a place that you have visited to write about. Think about the words you will use to describe the place. Write the name of the place in the center of a word web. Write five words or phrases that describe the place on the spokes.

A student named Linda listed her ideas in this word web:

beach sparkled in bright sunlight

sharp smell of salt water

cold ocean water, roaring waves

Beach

wet, smooth sand

amazing day

❷ Draft

Use your word web to help you write a first draft.

- Keep in mind your purpose for writing—to describe.
- Use words to show how the place looked or smelled and what you thought or how you felt about the place.

❸ Revise

Read over your draft. Look for places where the sentences begin the same way or the writing is not interesting. Use the Writing Checklist to help you identify problems. Then revise your draft.

❹ Edit

Check your work for errors. Trade papers with a partner to get feedback. Use the Peer Review Checklist on page 402.

❺ Publish

Prepare a clean copy of your final draft. Share your paragraph with the class. Save your work. You will need to refer to it in the Writing Workshop.

Here is Linda's description:

Writing Checklist

Ideas

✓ I created an exciting word picture of the place.

✓ I described how I felt and thought about the place.

Conventions

✓ I used regular past tense verbs correctly.

Linda Wu

Last summer my family visited a beautiful beach near our home. When we got closer to the ocean, I recognized the sharp smell of the salt water. As soon as we arrived, my sisters and I jumped from the car and raced along the shore. The beach sparkled in the bright sunlight. Then we rushed into the cold ocean water. Suddenly the roaring waves carried us back to shore. To warm up, we buried our feet under the wet, smooth sand. What an amazing day!

WB
31–32

Apply and Extend

Link the Readings

Copy the chart into your notebook.
Read the words in the top row.

- For *Taking Care of the Young*, put an X under the words that remind you of the selection.

- Repeat the same activity for the other readings.

	Informational text	Literature	Animals helping others	People helping others
Taking Care of the Young				
The Star Llama				
Mustangs				

Discussion

1. Why doesn't the clown fish stay with its young like other animal parents do?

2. How is the star llama different from the llamas the boy buys at the end of the story?

3. How does Wild Horse Annie's **challenge** remind you of how animal parents protect their young?

 How do animals and people show they care?

Listening Skills

If you want to hear something a speaker said again, you can say, "Would you repeat that, please?"

Projects

Your teacher will help you choose one of these projects.

Written	Oral	Visual/Active
Science Article	**Presentation**	**Picture Book**
Research an animal. Write information about how that animal cares for its young. Include pictures or photographs from magazines.	Prepare a lesson to share what you learned about an animal and its young. Present your lesson to classmates.	Create a picture book. Find photos that show how human parents and animal parents are similar.
Adventure Story	**Interview**	**Animal Playing Cards**
Write a story about a young animal that gets into trouble. Tell how its parent saves it. Make sure your story is based on facts about the animal.	Interview someone who has a pet. Find out how that person cares for the animal. Record your interview.	Create matching cards: one set for adult animals; the other for their young. Write the animal names. Use your cards to play games.

Further Reading

 For more projects visit
LongmanCornerstone.com

Beauty and the Beast, Paul Shipton
In this Penguin Young Reader®, an ugly beast teaches a beautiful woman a lesson about caring. Then her love changes the beast into a handsome prince.

Safe, Warm, and Snug, Stephen R. Swinburne
This is a rhyming text that tells about fascinating ways animals protect their young. Featured animals include kangaroos, emperor penguins, and bats.

WB
33–34

Play a Description Guessing Game

You are going to describe how animal parents care for their young. Then you will listen as your classmates talk about how animal parents care for their young.

❶ Prepare

A. Choose an animal. You will describe in five or more sentences how the parents take care of their young without naming the animal. Your classmates will have to guess the animal you are describing. You can decide if you need to use formal or informal language.

B. Write down some details to use in your description. It may help to reread the selections in the unit to find information and details for your description.

> These parents have one baby at a time. The baby is very, very small when it is born. The mother keeps it warm and safe in her pouch. The baby leaves its mother's pouch when it gets bigger. The baby jumps back into the pouch when there is danger.

❷ Practice

Practice your description in front of your family or friends. If possible, record your description. Then listen to yourself. How do you sound? Record yourself again and try to improve.

❸ Present

As you speak, do the following:

- Speak clearly and loudly enough for everyone to hear.
- Don't be nervous. Have fun. Remember, this is a game.

As you listen, do the following:

- Listen quietly to your classmates. Don't call out any guesses until your classmates ask for them.
- If you don't understand something a speaker says, you can say, "Excuse me. Could you repeat that, please?"

> **Speaking Skills**
>
> Include important details. This helps your listener picture what you are describing. You can use informal or formal language in your descriptions.

❹ Evaluate

After you speak, answer these questions:

- ✓ Did you understand the game rules?
- ✓ Did you choose important details?
- ✓ Did you say at least five sentences?

After you listen, answer these questions:

- ✓ Did you guess the animal?
- ✓ If you were describing how this animal cares for its young, would you have described it the same way? What details would you have included?
- ✓ Did the speaker use formal or informal language?

> **Listening Skills**
>
> Listen carefully for important words and details.

Writing Workshop

Write a Descriptive Essay

Writing Prompt

Write an essay that describes a memorable event. Use sensory details, or details that appeal to any of the five senses, to give your reader a mental picture of your description.

❶ Prewrite G.O. 149

Review the writing you have done in this unit. Then choose a topic. Think about school or community events that you have enjoyed. What sights, sounds, tastes, and smells did you experience? List your ideas in a graphic organizer.

> **Listening Skills**
>
> Writing an essay is a process. Listen carefully to your teacher's instructions and requests.

A student named Alex listed his ideas in this chart:

sight	sound	taste	touch	smell
crowded street	salsa music, people clapping	tangy mustard, fresh tomatoes	soft angora blankets	spicy stews freshly baked bread

❷ Draft

Use your graphic organizer to write a draft.

- Keep your purpose in mind—to describe an event.
- Use sensory details in your description.

❸ Revise

Read your draft. Look for places where the writing needs improvement. Use the Writing Checklist to help you. Then revise your draft.

Here is how Alex revised his essay:

Six Traits of Writing Checklist

✔ **Ideas**
Did I include sensory details?

✔ **Organization**
Are my ideas presented in order?

✔ **Voice**
Does my writing show energy and feeling?

✔ **Word Choice**
Did I choose specific words?

✔ **Sentence Fluency**
Did I vary my sentence lengths?

✔ **Conventions**
Did I use past tense verbs correctly?

Alex Romero

The Street Fair

Last Saturday my sister and I spent the day at a street fair. We strolled along the street and looked at all the interesting items for sale. The crowded street was lined with stalls selling everything from roasted corn to baby-soft angora blankets.

Revised to make the meaning clearer.

When we turned the corner, the excited beat of a salsa band greeted us. Immediately, people started dancing. They twirled their partners and They clapped their hands. My sister and I had to join in the fun.

Revised to combine sentences.

After dancing for a while, we stopped at a stall for lunch. The smells of spicy, hot stew and freshly baked bread reminded us that we were hungry. My sister tried the stew and I had a cheese sandwich with tangy mustard and fresh tomatoes.

Revised to combine sentences.

By evening we left the sights and sounds of the street far behind us. It was a great afternoon. I can not wait till next year!

Revised to correct spelling error.

❹ Edit

Check your work for errors. Trade papers with a partner. Use the Peer Review Checklist to give each other feedback. Edit your final draft in response to feedback from your partner and your teacher.

❺ Publish

Prepare a clean copy of your final draft. Share your essay with the class.

35–36

SPELLING TIP

You cannot form the past tense of irregular verbs by adding -ed to the end of the word.

blow ⟶ blew

say ⟶ said

Listen to the sentences. Pay attention to the groups of words. Read aloud.

1. Different kinds of animals try to keep their young secure.

2. A boy cares for his llama, and his llama companion helps him in return.

3. Two million mustangs once roamed free in the American West, but today we need to help them keep safe.

Work in pairs. Take turns reading the passage below aloud for one minute. Count the number of words you read.

Human babies and animal babies need adults to protect them.	10
Mother wallabies have an unusual way to protect their babies.	20
They carry their babies in a pouch. A baby wallaby, called a	32
joey, has no fur when it is born. The baby climbs into its	45
mother's pouch to stay warm. The wallaby's pouch also guards	55
the joey from danger.	59
When a joey gets older, it will sometimes leave its mother's	70
pouch. But mother wallabies still try to keep their babies	80
safe. If a mother wallaby senses trouble, she stomps on the	91
ground. This tells her joey to return to her pouch.	101

With your partner, find the words that slowed you down.

- Practice saying each word and then say the sentence each word is in.

- Take turns reading the text again. Count the number of words you read.

37–38

Test Preparation

Taking Tests

You will often take tests that help show what you know.
Follow these tips to improve your test-taking skills.

Coaching Corner

Answering Test Items That Are Cloze Items

- Cloze items ask you to fill in a blank.

- Sometimes you will be asked to complete a sentence. Other times you will be given a selection with some words left out.

- First read the questions and answer choices. Sometimes there is no question, just a list of words.

- Read the entire selection carefully. Try to think of words that might fit in the blanks as you read.

- If you don't know what a word means, use the words around it to help you.

- Silently, read the cloze with each answer choice. Then choose the answer that makes the most sense.

Read the following test sample. Study the tips in the box.

39–40

Read the selection. Then choose the correct words to fill in the blanks.

I spent a week at the Old River Ranch last summer. Mr. and Mrs. Lopez treated us like we really worked there. They had animals like horses, cattle, chickens, and pigs on the ranch. Each morning, we woke up very early to help feed all the __1__. I liked watching the __2__ colt the best. It was days-old and still very wobbly. It looked a little nervous. The colt stood right next to its mother so she could __3__ it. I hope I can spend some __4__ on a ranch again. It was great!

1 A geese
   B livestock
   C chicks
   D colts

2 F warm
   G young
   H feral
   J banned

3 A protect
   B shimmer
   C capture
   D recover

4 F work
   G food
   H time
   J money

Tips

 Look through the selection to figure out the answer.

 Be careful. Make sure you read the whole passage before choosing your answers.

Powerful Forces of Nature

Thunder and lightning! Floods! Hurricanes and erupting volcanoes! Powerful forces of nature change our world.

Reading

1 | Nonfiction

Vesuvius Erupts!

2 | Article

Thunder and Lightning

3 | Short Story

Hurricane!

THE BIG QUESTION

How do people protect themselves from powerful forces of nature?

Listening and Speaking

You will discuss the powerful forces of nature and what to do in an emergency. In the Listening and Speaking Workshop, you will give a how-to presentation.

Writing

You will practice expository writing. In the Writing Workshop, you will write a how-to essay.

Quick Write

Use a T-chart to compare a stormy day and a nice day.

DVD **VIEW AND RESPOND**
Talk about the poster for this unit. Then watch and listen to the video and answer the questions at LongmanCornerstone.com.

What do you know about weather?

Words to Know

Listen and repeat. Use these words to talk about weather.

 sunny

 snowy

 cloudy

 rainy

 windy

 foggy

 **Practice**

Work with a partner. Ask questions using the words above. Answer them using the words from the box or your own ideas.

summer	fall	winter	spring

Example: A: When is the weather <u>rainy</u>?

B: It is <u>rainy</u> in the <u>spring</u>.

Write

Read the questions. Write your response in your notebook.

What kind of weather do you like? Why?

Make Connections

Copy the sentences below into your notebook. Complete the sentences with the following words.

a blizzard

a hurricane

a flood

1. During _____ it is very windy and rainy. Sometimes trees could fall down. In some places in the United States, these could happen in June through December.

2. When there is too much rain in a bad storm or the river overflows with water, there could be _____.

3. There is a lot of snow in _____. It could also be very windy too. Most of these take place in the winter.

What about you?

Talk with a partner. Which one is the scariest—a flood, a hurricane, or a blizzard? Why?

Kids' Stories from around the World 🔊 Audio

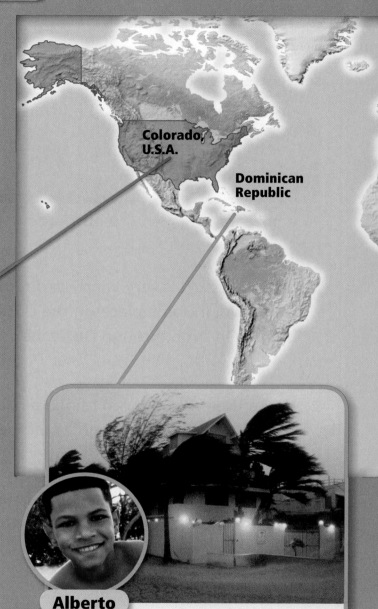

Colorado, U.S.A.

Dominican Republic

Jennifer

I live in Colorado, in the United States. Last year we had a very strong blizzard. Our lights went out, and our car was buried in snow. Our house became cold, and we needed food. We had to go to the local high school to get warm and to get something to eat.

Alberto

I live in the Dominican Republic. My country is part of an island in the Caribbean Sea. Almost every year the island is hit by powerful hurricanes. You shouldn't go outside during hurricanes. They are very dangerous.

Japan

Bangladesh

Atsuo

In Japan we sometimes have typhoons. Typhoons can cause flooding and mudslides because of heavy rains and very strong winds. They can destroy roads, houses, and trees. It is important to be prepared for this kind of emergency.

Bani

We have many floods in Bangladesh. In the spring, the snow on the mountains melts. We also have lots of rainstorms in my country. Our rivers often fill with too much water. The floods destroy towns and crops.

What about you?

1. What kind of weather do you have where you live?

2. Do you know of any stories about forces of nature? Share them with the class.

What You Will Learn

Reading
- Vocabulary building: *Context, word study*
- Reading strategy: *Predict*
- Text type: *Informational text (social studies)*

Grammar
Irregular past verbs

Writing
Organize ideas by cause and effect

These words will help you understand the reading.

Key Words

volcano

lava

crater

erupts

ash

Key Words

Vesuvius Erupts! is about a volcano that erupted almost 2,000 years ago.

Words in Context

1 A volcano is where melted rock, or lava, escapes through an opening in the Earth's surface.

2 The crater is the opening.

3 The lava erupts, or escapes, through the crater.

4 Ash, or tiny pieces of burned lava and gas, also escapes in a volcanic eruption.

Mount St. Helens is a volcano in Washington State. Its last large eruption was in 1980. ▼

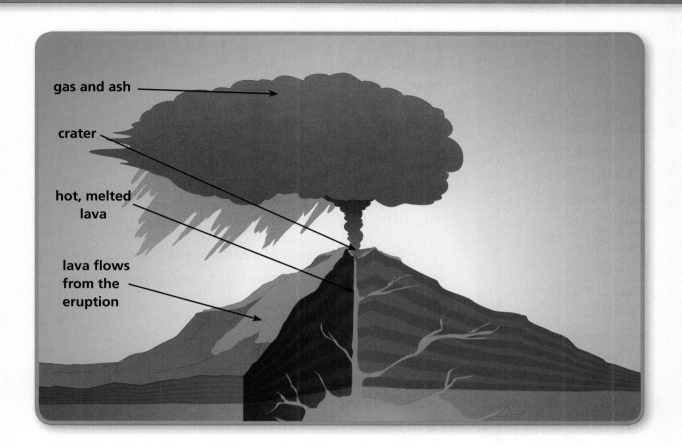

gas and ash

crater

hot, melted lava

lava flows from the eruption

Practice

Draw a picture of a volcano in your notebook. Label the picture using sentences that contain the key words.

Make Connections

An eruption usually occurs suddenly. Do you remember something that happened very suddenly? How did you feel? What did you do?

Speaking Skills

When you don't know the right word to use, explain or describe the idea using words you know.

WB
41

These words will help you talk about the reading.

Academic Words

consist of
made up of

evidence
proof

similar
almost the same, but not exactly

Academic Words

Words in Context Audio

Mud **consists of** soil and water.

The scientists found **evidence** that people lived near the volcano a long time ago.

The two mountains are **similar** in height, but one mountain is wider than the other one.

Practice

Write the sentences in your notebook. Choose an academic word to complete each sentence.

1. The wet grass is _____ that it rained last night.

2. The books _____ different stories about volcanoes.

3. Lions and pet cats are _____, but lions are very big and pet cats are small.

Apply

Ask and answer with a partner.

1. How are books and movies **similar**? How are they different?

2. What does a good lunch **consist of**?

3. Why is **evidence** important to scientists?

Word Study

Pronunciation of Ending -ed

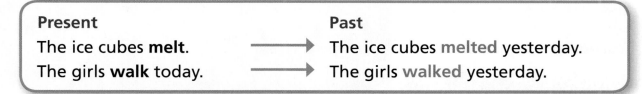

The words in red below name actions that happened in the past. They end in *-ed.* Listen. Then read the sentences aloud.

Present		Past
The ice cubes **melt**.	⟶	The ice cubes **melted** yesterday.
The girls **walk** today.	⟶	The girls **walked** yesterday.

Adding the *-ed* ending to *melt* adds a syllable.
Adding the *-ed* ending to *walk* does not add a syllable.

Rule

If the letter *t* or the letter *d* comes before the *-ed* ending, then *-ed* is pronounced as a separate syllable.

Practice

Work with a partner. Sound out the words in the box.

melted	stayed
filled	decided
started	waited
called	helped

- Copy the words.

- Circle the word if the *-ed* adds another syllable.

- Cross out the word if the *-ed* does not add another syllable.

- Take turns reading the words aloud.

- List other words that end in *-ed.* Have your partner tell if the *-ed* adds another syllable.

43

INFORMATIONAL TEXT

Literary Nonfiction

More About

How can past events teach us how to protect ourselves?

Listen to the Audio.
Listen for the general meaning. Use the pictures to help you understand the selection.

Reading Strategy

Predict

Before you read, guess, or predict, what the story will be about. Follow these steps:

- Read the title.
- Look at the illustrations and photos. Read the captions.
- Predict what the story will be about.

Listen as your teacher models the reading strategy.

Vesuvius Erupts!

The Temple of Isis was in Pompeii.

Pompeii was a city on the Bay of Naples.

POMPEII, 79 C.E.

It was a very hot morning in Pompeii. Even Mount Vesuvius gave no **shade** to the city below.

Hot weather did not stop the people of Pompeii. They walked in the streets and shopped in the markets. The smell of bread from a bakery filled the air. Musicians played and sang for the shoppers.

At a restaurant, two women ordered food. A man tied his dog to a tree. Just then, the ground began to shake. The dog barked. It was scared.

---

shade   area that gets little sun

Pompeii was a busy town.

Before You Go On | What were some people doing the morning Vesuvius erupted?

People stopped talking. The women looked worried. Was it an **earthquake?**

Boom! Suddenly, the top of Mount Vesuvius blew off! Now the mountain had a crater. The volcano was erupting. Fire and huge black clouds rose into the sky. The ground was shaking. People ran from their homes.

Ash and smoke covered the sun. Daytime turned into darkness. Lava poured down the mountain. Hot ash and rocks fell from the sky.

The ash covered people's heads, faces, and bodies. It burned their eyes. It filled their mouths as they called for help. The air became very thick with ash and gases. It was hard to breathe.

The ash piled higher and higher. Soon, it blocked the streets. Roofs **collapsed** because the ash and rocks were so heavy. The ash filled the rooms. Pompeii was disappearing. Soon, the ash buried the city.

---

earthquake   sudden shaking of the Earth

collapsed   fell down

The House of the Great Fountain was found in Pompeii.

This is a wall painting in Pompeii of the goddess Flora.

About 2,000 people stayed in the city. Some chose to stay. Others were trapped. All of them died. But 20,000 people were able to escape.

In less than two days, ash and rocks buried the city. Heavy rain made the ash hard like cement. Pompeii stayed buried for almost 1,700 years!

In about 1750, the King of Naples ordered workers to uncover Pompeii. They started to dig through the rocks. They found the city almost exactly as it was when the volcano erupted.

The eruption of Vesuvius was a **tragic** event. But it also taught us about life long ago. Many people and objects were frozen in time. As a result, today we know much about how people lived almost 2,000 years ago.

Workers still dig in the ruins of Pompeii.

---

tragic sad

44–46

Reading Strategy

Predict

Before reading, you predicted what the story would be about.

- Were your predictions correct?
- Did making predictions help you to understand the story? How?

Think It Over

1. **Recall** During the eruption what did the air **consist of**?

2. **Comprehend** How is a volcanic eruption **similar** to an earthquake? Explain.

3. **Analyze** What can we learn from the **evidence** that was uncovered in Pompeii?

Vesuvius and Pompeii

▲ Aerial photo
This aerial photo of the crater was taken from an airplane.

▲ Burned bread
Workers found 81 loaves of bread.

▲ Roman city
Pompeii is in Italy. The people who lived on these narrow streets were Romans.

▲ Victims

Many of the victims were farmers. The soil on Vesuvius was very rich. The farmers were not afraid of the volcano. It had been quiet for years!

▲ Bay of Naples

Vesuvius is on the coast of the Bay of Naples.

▲ Ruins

Today, people from all over the world visit the ruins at Pompeii.

Activity to Do

These two pages tell you more about Pompeii.

- Choose another city.
- Research the city online or in the library.
- Create two pages, using pictures and words, to tell about the city.

Learning Strategies

Sequence of Events

In many stories, events happen in a certain order. This order is called the **sequence** of events.

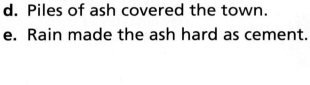

Practice

Read this series of events from *Vesuvius Erupts!* List the events in the order in which they happened.

a. Pompeii stayed buried for hundreds of years.

b. Vesuvius erupted.

c. People in Pompeii started an ordinary day.

d. Piles of ash covered the town.

e. Rain made the ash hard as cement.

Use a Sequence of Events Chart

A Sequence of Events Chart can help you summarize the main events in a story in the order they happened.

Answer the questions below to complete the Sequence of Events Chart.

1. Which event would you add to the middle of the chart?
   a. Women talked at a restaurant.
   b. Pompeii was buried by ash in less than two days.
   c. The King of Naples gave an order.
   d. People shopped in the markets.

2. Which sentence could be added to the end of the chart?
   a. Workers began to uncover Pompeii.
   b. About 2,000 people stayed in town.
   c. Huge black clouds blocked the sun.
   d. Two women ordered food.

Retell the selection to a partner.
Use some of the key words.

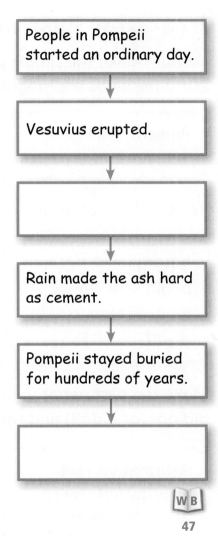

Extension

Utilize Suppose you wanted people in the future to know about your life. Find **evidence** that tells about your life. Share it with your class. Tell why you chose it.

Grammar

Irregular Past Verbs

You can make the **simple past tense** of most verbs by adding -*ed.*
But some verbs are **irregular**. You do not add -*ed* to these verbs.

Present   **Past**
People **run** from their homes.   ⟶   People **ran** from their homes.

Review these **common irregular verbs**.

become ⟶ became   fall ⟶ fell   make ⟶ made
begin ⟶ began   find ⟶ found   rise ⟶ rose
blow ⟶ blew   give ⟶ gave   run ⟶ ran
choose ⟶ chose   have ⟶ had   sing ⟶ sang

Make the past **negative** form of irregular verbs with
did not (or *didn't*) and the plain form of the verb.

did not = **didn't**

Affirmative Past   **Negative Past**
They **found** the city.   ⟶   They **did not find** the city.

Make *Yes-No* **questions** and *Wh-***questions** with *did* and the
plain form of the verb when there is a subject. When there is
no subject in a *Wh-question,* use the past form of the verb.

Did they **find** the city?
Where **did** they **find** the city?
Who **found** the city?

Change each irregular verb to the past tense. Write the sentences.

Example: The musicians sing a song.

The musicians sang a song.

1. The volcano begins to erupt.

2. Rocks and ash fall from the sky.

3. Some people choose to stay.

4. Rocks and ash make the city disappear.

5. Workers find **evidence** of the eruption.

Apply

Work with a partner. Ask and answer the questions about *Vesuvius Erupts!* If you need to, look back at the reading. Use regular and irregular past verbs in your answers.

Example: A: Did Vesuvius begin to erupt at night?

B: No. It began to erupt in the morning.

- Did Vesuvius begin to erupt at night?
- What happened to the top of Vesuvius?
- Did fire rise into the sky?
- Did people stay in their homes?
- Did houses fall from the sky?
- Did everyone choose to leave?
- What happened to the air?
- How did the rain make the ash hard like cement?
- When did the king's workers find Pompeii?

48

Grammar Check ✓

Name some irregular past verbs.

Writing

Organize Ideas by Cause and Effect

Ongoing Writing Skills Practice

Expository writing informs or explains. One way to organize expository writing is by cause and effect. A cause is something that makes something else happen. An effect is what happens as a result of the cause.

Writing Prompt

Write a paragraph explaining the causes and effects of an event. The event can be from real life or from books, movies, or television. Be sure to use irregular past verbs correctly.

❶ Prewrite

G.O. 148

Choose an event to write about. Ask yourself why things happened as they did. List the causes and effects in a graphic organizer.

A student named Barbara listed her ideas like this:

❷ Draft

Use your graphic organizer to write a draft.

- Explain the causes and effects of an event.
- Show how each cause leads to an effect.

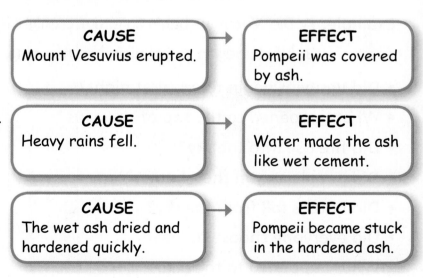

CAUSE
Mount Vesuvius erupted.

→

EFFECT
Pompeii was covered by ash.

CAUSE
Heavy rains fell.

→

EFFECT
Water made the ash like wet cement.

CAUSE
The wet ash dried and hardened quickly.

→

EFFECT
Pompeii became stuck in the hardened ash.

❸ Revise

Read your draft. Look for places where the writing needs improvement. Use the Writing Checklist to help you find problems. Then revise your draft.

❹ Edit

Check your work for errors. Trade papers with a partner. Use the Peer Review Checklist on page 402. Edit your final draft in response to feedback from your partner and your teacher.

❺ Publish

Make a clean copy of your final draft. Share it with the class. Save your work. You'll need to refer to it in the Writing Workshop at the end of the unit.

Here is Barbara's cause-and-effect paragraph:

Writing Checklist

Ideas

✔ I showed how causes led to effects.

✔ I expressed my ideas clearly.

Conventions

✔ I used irregular past verbs correctly.

Barbara Torres

The top of Mount Vesuvius blew off. Smoke filled the air. Ash fell from the sky, covering everything. Within two days, Pompeii was buried. Heavy rains fell. The rainwater mixed with the ash, making it like wet cement. The wet ash dried and hardened quickly. Everything in Pompeii was stuck in the hardened ash. The city stayed buried for hundreds of years. Workers began uncovering the city in 1750. The ash had preserved Pompeii! People and things were exactly as they were at the time of the eruption. It was frozen in time.

49–50

Prepare to Read

What You Will Learn

Reading

- Vocabulary building: *Context, word study*

- Reading strategy: *Identify genre*

- Text type: *Informational text (Internet article)*

Grammar

Imperatives and time-order transitions

Writing

Explain how to do something

These words will help you understand the reading.

Key Words

lightning

thunder

electricity

temperature

evaporate

Which of these three pictures show items that use electricity?

Key Words

You will read three passages about thunder and lightning. Each passage gives information in a different format.

Words in Context

Lightning is a flash of light in the sky. It happens during a storm. It is usually followed by a loud sound called thunder.

Electricity is a kind of energy. Lightning in the sky is electricity.

Temperature is a measure of how hot or cold something is.

When water gets hot, it boils. Then, water will evaporate and change into a vapor or gas.

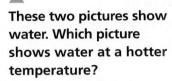

These two pictures show water. Which picture shows water at a hotter temperature?

Practice

Make flashcards to help you memorize the words.

- Write a key word on the front.
- On the back, write the meaning.

Make Connections

What things in your home use electricity? How are they important in your life?

These words will help you talk about the reading.

Academic Words

appropriate
fitting; suitable

demonstrate
show how to do something

feature
a part that stands out

Academic Words

Words in Context

It is **appropriate** to raise your hand when you ask a question in class.

The scientist is going to **demonstrate** how to create electricity.

The newspaper's photographic essays are one of its most interesting **features**.

Practice

Write the sentences in your notebook. Choose an academic word to complete each sentence.

1. The best _____ of the cell phone is the camera.
2. A firefighter came to our class to _____ what to do during a fire drill.
3. The new action movie is _____ for families and children.

Apply

Ask and answer with a partner.

1. What **feature** of your textbook do you like the best?
2. What are some **appropriate** ways to act in your classroom?
3. Can you **demonstrate** how to make a paper airplane? Show your partner.

Word Study

Compound Words

Sometimes, two words come together to form a new word. These new words are called **compound words**.

class + room = classroom

thunder + storm = thunderstorm

Rule

This is a pattern in English: look for the smaller words that make up a compound word. They can help you pronounce and understand the compound word. For example, **thunderstorm** is a storm with thunder.

Practice

Work with a partner. Copy the words below.

sunshine	lookout	daytime
flashlight	anywhere	raincoat

Reading Skill

Looking for patterns in English will make you a better reader.

- Circle all of the smaller words you see.
- Compare your list to your partner's. Did you find the same words?
- Add more compound words to your list.
- Read your lists aloud.

53

INFORMATIONAL TEXT

Internet Article

More About

What can you do to stay safe during thunder and lightning storms?

 Listen to the Audio.
Listen for the general meaning. Use the pictures to help you understand the selection.

Reading Strategy

Identify Genre

A genre is a type of writing. Stories, poems, articles, plays, and letters are some genres.

- What do you notice about the genres of the readings that follow?

Listen as your teacher models the reading strategy.

Thunder and Lightning

Electricity in the Sky

Lightning is a big **flash** of electricity. It is released during a storm. Lightning strikes more often in the summer than in the winter. That's because there are more storms in the summer. Sunny weather and hot temperature heat the air and make water evaporate. The hot air and water **vapor** rise into the sky. As they rise, they meet the cold air.

---

flash   sudden, bright light
vapor   small drops that float in the air

Cloud-to-cloud lightning

Up in the Clouds

The cold air makes the water vapor turn back into water **droplets** or ice **crystals**. That forms a cloud. Inside the cloud, the droplets and crystals carry a tiny bit of electricity. The electricity builds until lightning suddenly forms.

Lightning can jump from one cloud to another (see image 1). It can move from a cloud to the ground (see image 2). Sometimes lightning can even move from the ground up to a cloud (see image 3).

Lightning is five times hotter than the sun. Lightning heats the air around it so quickly that the air explodes. Thunder is the noise we hear when the air explodes.

Cloud-to-ground lightning

Catch Me If You Can!

Light moves faster than sound. This means we see the flash of lightning before we hear the thunder. It takes five seconds for the noise of the thunder to go one mile. If you see lightning and then hear thunder five seconds later, the storm is one mile away. If thunder comes ten seconds after lightning, the storm is two miles away.

Ground-to-cloud lightning

droplets   very small drops of liquid
crystals   little pieces of ice

Before You Go On   Why do we see lightning before we hear the thunder?

Staying Safe
in a Lightning Storm

Lightning can be dangerous.
Here are some tips to stay safe.

Outdoors

1. Check if thunderstorms are in the **forecast**.
2. Find shelter in a strong building or in a car with a hard roof.
3. Do not stand under trees that are alone in the middle of a field.
   Do not stand under tall trees when there are shorter trees close by.
4. Do not stand near things that are made of metal.

Indoors

1. Close all the windows and doors.
2. Do not use the telephone.
3. Do not take a bath or shower. Stay away from water.
4. Turn off electrical appliances, including computers and TVs.

The Lightning Crouch

If you feel your skin tingle or your hair stand up, this could mean you are about to be hit by lightning. Get into the "Lightning Crouch." Crouch down low and curl into a small ball. Put your hands on your knees, and keep your head down. Try to be as small as you can, with very little touching the ground. DO NOT LIE ON THE GROUND!

---

forecast   description of weather that is likely to occur in the future

November 12, 2011

Dear Grandma,

Thank you for your letter. I am sorry you had a bad day. Maybe it will make you feel better to know about Roy C. Sullivan. I just read about some bad luck he had. He was struck by lightning more times than anyone else in the world! From 1942 to 1977, he was struck seven different times by lightning!

Roy worked in a national park. He was standing on a high tower in the park when he was first hit with lightning. Years later, he was driving along a road when lightning struck him again. Lightning hit him five more times.

Roy was unlucky, but he was also lucky. It's very dangerous to be struck by lightning. He was never badly hurt, though.

You and I can be even luckier than Roy. At school I learned how to protect myself from being struck by lightning. I'll tell you how in my next letter.

Love,
Emilio

54–56

Reading Strategy

Identify Genre

- What are some **features** of a scientific article?
- How was reading Emilio's letter different from reading the Internet article?
- Ask your teacher or classmates if you don't understand how to identify genres.

Think It Over

1. **Recall** How can you **demonstrate** the lightning crouch?
2. **Comprehend** What are the **appropriate** actions to take when you are indoors during a lightning storm?
3. **Analyze** Why was Roy C. Sullivan more lucky than unlucky? Explain.

Learning Strategies

Compare Genres

Genres have different purposes and are organized in different ways.

Informational Articles are usually organized into paragraphs and have a title and headings. An article often has photographs or illustrations to make the facts clearer.

How-to Posters often have headings and numbered steps. The headings help you find information. The numbered steps tell the order you should follow.

Friendly Letters have a date, a salutation (Dear Grandma), a message, and a closing (Love, Emilio).

Practice

Copy the chart below. Write *article*, *poster*, or *letter* in the final column. There can be more than one answer.

November 12, 2011

Dear Grandma,
Thank you for your letter. I am sorry you had a bad day. Maybe it will make you feel better to know about Roy C. Sullivan. I just read about some bad luck he had. He was struck by lightning more times than anyone else in the world! From 1942 to 1977, he was struck seven different times by lightning!
Roy worked in a national park. He was standing on a high tower in the park when he was first hit with lightning. Years later, he was driving along a road when lightning struck him again. Lightning hit him five more times.
Roy was unlucky, but he was also lucky. It's very dangerous to be struck by lightning. He was never badly hurt, though.
You and I can be even luckier than Roy. At school I learned how to protect myself from being struck by lightning. I'll tell you how in my next letter.

Love,
Emilio

Statements	Genre
1. **Purpose:** It is written to one person.	letter
2. **Purpose:** It is written to present information to many people.	
3. **Headings:** It has headings.	
4. **Numbered Steps:** It has steps that tell what order to follow.	
5. **Information:** It tells facts.	

Use a Venn Diagram

A Venn Diagram makes it easy to see what is the same or different about two items. Circle A represents one item. Circle B represents another. The part that overlaps represents things that are true for both.

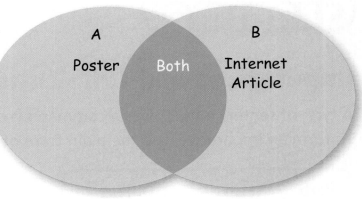

A   Poster   Both   B   Internet Article

Create a Venn Diagram to compare two of the genres. Use the statements from the chart on the previous page.

- Choose two of the three genres from the selection.
- Draw a blank Venn Diagram. List one genre in Circle A. List the other genre in Circle B.
- Write statements that are true for one genre, but not for the other genre, in the big parts of Circle A or Circle B.
- Write statements that both genres have in common in the section labeled *Both*.

57

Take notes about the selection.

- Share them with a partner.
- Try to use the key words.

Extension

Utilize Work in small groups. Make a poster warning people about a danger. Do research. Share the information with your group. Be sure to listen carefully to your classmates and work cooperatively.

Grammar

Imperatives and Time-Order Transitions

A type of sentence that gives a command is called an **imperative**.
To form an imperative, use the plain form of the verb plus an object.

Verb		Object
Close	⟶	the door.

To make a negative imperative, use *Do not* plus the plain form
of the verb and an object.

Verb		Object
Do not use	⟶	the telephone.

We often use imperatives to give instructions. **Time-order
transition words** are connecting words that order sentences
to lead us step-by-step to a conclusion. Notice how the words
break up a task into a beginning, middle, and end.

> **Time-Order Transition Words**
> First, crouch down low.
> Then, curl into a ball.
> Next, put your hands on your knees.
> Finally, do not touch the ground!

Time-order transition words can be used to combine phrases and sentences.

> As soon as you crouch down low, immediately curl into a ball.
> Meanwhile, do not touch the ground until the storm passes.

Practice

The sentences below describe how to count lightning. Copy the sentences, then write a number next to each one to put the steps in order. Then circle the time-order transition words.

Example: _1_ (First,) you need to see the lightning flash.

_____ First, you need to see the lightning flash.

_____ Then, keep counting while you listen for the thunder.

_____ Immediately after you see the flash, begin to count seconds slowly.

_____ Finally, divide the number of seconds by five.

_____ As soon as you hear the thunder, stop counting.

Apply

Work with a partner. Choose an activity from the list below. Explain how to do it to a partner. Your partner will repeat your directions. Then switch roles.

58

Example: A: Train a dog to shake hands. First, you need some snacks.

B: Next, tell the dog to sit.

- Train a pet
- Make a snack
- Tie your shoes
- Play a game
- Draw a funny face
- Make a paper airplane
- Play an instrument

Grammar Check ✓

What are some time-order transition words?

Writing

Explain How to Do Something

Ongoing
Writing
Skills
Practice

Writers explain how to do something in clear, step-by-step instructions. The verbs are in the command form. The steps are written in correct time-order. Often the writers introduce each step with time-order words, such as *first, next, then,* and *last.*

Writing Prompt

Write a paragraph that explains how to do or make something. Explain the steps in the correct order from first to last. Be sure to use the command form of verbs and time-order words.

❶ Prewrite G.O. 144

Choose a topic to write about, such as how to care for a pet or prepare a recipe. List the steps to follow in a Sequence of Events Chart.

A student named Juan listed his ideas in this Sequence of Events Chart:

❷ Draft

Use your sequence of events chart to help you write a first draft.

- Keep in mind your purpose for writing—to explain.
- Show the steps in clear order, from first to last.

> **STEP 1:**
> Cut hole in shoebox lid and glue four toothpicks on lid.

> **STEP 2:**
> Slide two thick and two thin rubber bands around shoe box, across hole.

> **STEP 3:**
> Slide pencil under four rubber bands, at the end of box near the hole.

❸ Revise

Read over your draft. Look for places where the writing is unclear and the steps are not in the correct order. Use the Writing Checklist to help you identify problems. Then revise your draft.

❹ Edit

Check your work for errors. Trade papers with a partner to get feedback. Use the Peer Review Checklist on page 402. Edit your final draft in response to feedback from your partner.

❺ Publish

Prepare a clean copy of your final draft. Share your paragraph with the class. Save your work.

Here is Juan's paragraph:

Writing Checklist

Ideas

✓ I clearly explained each step in the instructions.

Organize

✓ I arranged the steps in order from first to last.

Conventions

✓ I used imperatives and time-order transitions.

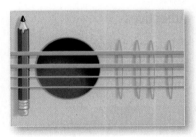

Juan Tadeo

First, cut a hole near one end of a shoebox lid. Then glue four toothpicks on the lid. Space the toothpicks evenly between the hole and the other end of the lid. Slide the two thickest rubber bands around the shoe box, so they go across the hole in the lid. Then slide the two thinnest rubber bands around the box in the same way. Finally, slide the pencil under the four rubber bands. Put the pencil at the very end of the box near the hole you cut. Now play the guitar by plucking the rubber bands.

59–60

What You Will Learn

Reading

- Vocabulary building: *Context, phonics*
- Reading strategy: *Visualize setting*
- Text type: *Literature (short story)*

Grammar
Adjectives

Explain a Process
Write a response to literature

These words will help you understand the reading.

Key Words

breeze

hurricane

shelter

bolt

Key Words

Hurricane! is a story about a family on vacation who lived through a hurricane.

Words in Context

1 A breeze is a light wind. When it is breezy, plants and trees may move a little.

2 A hurricane is a big tropical storm. It brings very strong winds and a large amount of rain.

3 When a hurricane is coming, people can go to a shelter. A shelter is a place where people are protected from forces of nature.

4 A bolt of lightning looks like a white line in the sky.

Practice

Add a page to your vocabulary notebook.

- Divide your page into three columns: the new words, their definitions, and drawings of the words when possible.
- Test yourself by covering one of the columns.

Make Connections

What was the biggest storm you ever lived through? Discuss this question with a partner. Use the key words. Then write your response in your notebook.

61

These words will help you talk about the reading.

Academic Words

assistance
help or support

impact
a strong effect

major
big; very important or serious

Academic Words

Words in Context Audio

Emergency workers give **assistance** to people who are hurt.

Hurricanes cause a lot of damage and have a huge **impact** on a town.

Some people must leave their homes before a **major** storm comes.

Practice

Write the sentences in your notebook. Choose an academic word to complete each sentence.

1. Going to a new school is a _____ change.
2. The student needs _____ because his bag is very heavy.
3. The new president had a big _____ on the country.

Apply

Ask and answer with a partner.

1. What are some **major** storms you know about?
2. What **impact** could a storm have?
3. What kinds of **assistance** might people need in a storm?

Phonics

Digraphs: *ch, sh, th*

Sometimes two letters combine to make one sound. The letters *ch*, *sh*, and *th* are examples. These letters can come anywhere in a word. Listen. Sound out the words in the box.

ch	*sh*	*th*
chances	share	think
cheer	shelter	this
approaching	shore	thunder
watched	flash	weather
beach	splashed	with

Practice

Work with a partner. Take turns.

- Choose a word from the chart. Say the word aloud.
- Without looking at the word, have your partner tell whether the word has the letters *ch*, *sh*, or *th*.
- List six more words that are spelled with *ch*, *sh*, or *th*.

63

Short Story

More About

THE BIG QUESTION

Why is it important to know about dangerous weather?

Audio **Listen to the Audio.**
Listen for the general meaning. Use the pictures to help you understand the story.

Reading Strategy

Visualize Setting

The setting of this story is important. As you read *Hurricane!*, picture each new setting in your mind.

- Think about how the author describes the setting.
- Look for descriptive words.

Listen as your teacher models the reading strategy.

HURRICANE!

by Tracey Baptiste
illustrated by Amy Huntington

We went to the beach for our summer vacation. I splashed in the clear, blue sea. Mom and Dad sat on the shore. It was sunny, but not for long.

A man ran toward us. He worked at a nearby hotel.

"Señor! Señorita!" he called. "A big storm is coming. You must leave the beach now!" He told us that a hurricane was **approaching**. Everyone had to go to a shelter.

---

approaching   moving nearer

"But the water is so nice," I said sadly.
"Hurricanes are dangerous. We must leave," Dad said.

Mom smiled to make me feel better. Just then, I felt a breeze. Suddenly, the wind grew stronger and sand flew all around the beach.

"Let's go!" Dad said.

Before You Go On

What **impact** did the storm have on the people on the beach?

Mom and I packed all of our bags. Dad nailed wood over the windows of the beach house. This would **protect** the house from wind and rain.

"Our vacation is **ruined**," I cried.

"Maybe the storm won't last for long," Mom said. "But we can't take chances. We have to go where it is safe."

"We'll be OK," said Dad. "Think of this as an adventure."

I tried to cheer up. I might have an exciting story to tell my friends. But soon my adventure did not seem to be so fun.

The hurricane came closer. Lightning flashed! I saw a bolt of lightning over the water. Thunder clapped! Rain fell like sheets of glass from the sky. It was hard to see out of the car windows.

---

protect shield from danger

ruined spoiled or destroyed

"The streets will flood soon," Dad said.

"We must drive carefully," Mom said.

The shore was pounded by angry waves. The waves were strong and high. It was the afternoon, but the sky was as dark as night.

People on the **coast** were leaving their homes. The roads were crowded with cars. Our car moved slowly down the wet road.

---

coast   where the land meets the ocean

Before You Go On   What kind of **major** damage can a storm do?

Later that day, we stopped at a hotel. Usually, people on vacation stayed there. Now it was a shelter for travelers. Many people were in the lobby of the hotel. They were caught by the storm. They had nowhere else to go.

Mom and I watched the news on TV. The weather **forecaster** talked about the storm. She explained that soon it would be over. But some people were **trapped**. They were caught by the fast storm.

But my family was warm and safe inside the shelter. Outside, the wind and rain shook the trees and windows. People who were still outside needed help.

---

forecaster   person who tells what the weather will be like

trapped   not able to get out

Reading Skill

The word *fine* is a basic sight word. It's a word you recognize automatically. You don't have to sound it out.

One news reporter was in a boat. He saw a family on a raft. Their house was **flooded**, but they were fine. Emergency teams **rescued** these people. By that night, everyone was safe. I was happy now. And I had a story to share.

---

flooded   covered in water

rescued   helped or saved

64–66

Reading Strategy

Visualize Setting

- Describe the setting in your own words.

- Could this story have happened where you live? Why or why not?

- Did visualizing the setting help you to understand the story? How?

Think It Over

1. **Recall**   Where does this story take place?

2. **Comprehend**   How did the hotel offer **assistance** to the travelers?

3. **Analyze**   What **impact** did the hurricane have on this family's vacation?

Learning Strategies

Clues to Setting

To understand a story better, it helps to form a picture in your mind of the setting. The **setting** is where and when a story takes place. The setting of *Hurricane!* is near the beach during a hurricane.

Practice

Work with a partner. Look for clues to the setting.

- Reread pages 108–109.

- Copy the words, phrases, or sentences that help you get a clear picture of the setting of the story.

Use a Word Web

A Word Web helps you create a picture in your mind using just words.

Copy and complete this Word Web to describe the setting of *Hurricane!*

1. Read the questions in each circle.
2. Write in each circle what you visualize, or picture, in your mind.
3. Compare your Word Web with your partner's. How are they alike? How are they different?

Using the pictures in the story, make an outline of the events. Then narrate the story to a partner.

Extension

Utilize A setting can be drawn or even built in a model. Think of a setting that you know well. Picture how it might look during a big storm. Bring your setting to life in a description, drawing, or model. Share your setting with your class.

W B
67

Grammar

Adjectives

Adjectives are words that describe (or modify) nouns. They answer the questions *Which? Whose?* or *What kind?* Usually an adjective comes before the noun it describes. An adjective can also come after the noun following the *be* verb.

Adjective	Noun
It was a **big**	**balloon**.

Noun	Adjective
The **balloon**	was **big**.

Different types of adjectives describe different qualities.
Purpose adjectives often end in *-ing*, like *sleeping bag, frying pan*, and *swimming pool*.

Type	Adjective	Noun
opinion	**beautiful**	bird
size	**small**	desk
color	**red**	umbrella
material – what it's made of	**brick**	house
purpose – what it's used for	**sleeping**	bag

Sometimes we use more than one adjective before a noun. In that case, we list them in order by type, from opinion to purpose.

Adjective	Adjective	Noun
pretty (opinion)	blue (color)	flower
big (size)	wooden (material)	ship
metal (material)	frying (purpose)	pan

Practice

Add adjectives before each noun. If you need to, look back to the order of adjectives. Then write which type each adjective is.

Example: a _____ day at the beach

a <u>fun</u> day at the beach (opinion)

1. a _____ house (_____)

2. two _____ paintings (_____)

3. a _____ _____ bicycle (_____ , _____)

4. a _____ _____ bag (_____ , _____)

5. a _____ _____ storm (_____ , _____)

Apply

Work with a partner. Describe the things listed below. Use your five senses to describe each one. Use adjectives in your answers.

Example: A: A toy. A yo-yo is a small plastic toy.

B: A yo-yo has a long string. Yo-yos are fun.

- a toy
- an outdoor place
- a kind of weather
- a kind of food
- an animal or pet
- a family member

W B

68

Grammar Check ✓

Name each type of adjective listed in the table.

Writing

Explain a Process

Ongoing Writing Skills Practice

A process tells you how something happens. To explain a process, writers put the steps in order, from first to last. They include time-order words, such as *first*, *then*, *next*, and *last*. The steps in a process should be clear and include as many details as possible.

Writing Prompt

Write a paragraph that explains something you do in steps, such as growing a class plant or taking care of a pet. Be sure to use adjectives correctly.

❶ Prewrite

Choose a process to explain. Think about the steps that you follow. List the steps, from first to last, in a chart.

A student named Sandra listed her ideas in this chart:

❷ Draft

Use your chart to help you write a first draft.

- Keep in mind your purpose for writing—to explain.
- Present the information clearly and include as many details as possible.
- Include time-order words.

THE LIFE CYCLE OF A BUTTERFLY

STEP 1: Butterfly attaches egg to leaf or stem.

STEP 2: Long caterpillar feeds and grows. It has a pattern of stripes and patches on body. It sheds skin three or four times.

STEP 3: A pupa, or chrysalis, develops in a green or brown outer case, called a cocoon. Inside, the chrysalis turns into a butterfly.

STEP 4: Full-grown butterfly leaves the cocoon. It travels and lays eggs. Life cycle begins again.

❸ Revise

Read over your draft. Look for places where there are not enough details and the steps are not in the correct order. Use the Writing Checklist to help you identify problems. Then revise your draft.

❹ Edit

Check your work for errors in grammar, usage, mechanics, and spelling. Trade papers with a partner to get feedback. Use the Peer Review Checklist on page 402.

❺ Publish

Prepare a clean copy of your final draft. Share your paragraph with the class. Save your work. You will need to refer to it in the Writing Workshop.

Here is Sandra's explanation:

Writing Checklist

Ideas

✔ I wrote the steps in a process, from first to last.

✔ I expressed my ideas clearly and included details.

Conventions

✔ I included adjectives.

69–70

Sandra Miller

1. In the first stage, a butterfly attaches a tiny egg to a leaf or stem.
2. In the next stage, a long caterpillar develops. It has an interesting pattern of stripes on its body. The caterpillar feeds and grows. It sheds its outer skin three or four times.
3. In the third stage a pupa, or chrysalis, develops. It is wrapped in a tough green or brown outer case called a cocoon. The pupa turns into a butterfly.
4. Finally, a beautiful butterfly leaves the cocoon. This colorful butterfly will travel to new places. It will lay eggs and the life cycle will begin again.

Apply and Extend

Link the Readings

Copy the chart into your notebook. Read the words in the top row. Then follow these steps:

- For *Vesuvius Erupts!*, put an *X* under the words that remind you of the selection.

- Repeat the same activity for the other readings.

	Informational text	Literature	Events caused by nature	Events caused by a storm
Vesuvius Erupts!				
Thunder and Lightning				
Hurricane!				

Discussion

1. When Vesuvius erupted, the people of Pompeii were surprised. Do forces of nature today usually surprise people? Explain.

2. Describe the **impact** that the hurricane had on the town in *Hurricane!*

3. What is **similar** about volcanoes, thunder and lightning storms, hurricanes, and other **major** forces of nature?

 How do people protect themselves from powerful forces of nature?

Listening Skills

If someone is speakin too quickly, you can s; "Can you speak more slowly, please?"

Projects

Your teacher will help you choose one of these projects.

Written	Oral	Visual/Active
Safety Guidelines	**Folktale**	**World Map**
Research what to do during a storm. Write school guidelines for students to follow in case of a terrible storm.	Long ago, people created folktales to explain the weather. Tell your own folktale to explain a form of extreme weather.	Create a map of the world. Post photos on it showing types of extreme weather that are found around the world.
News Article	**Vocabulary Hunt**	**Graphic Organizer**
Research on the Internet or at the library to find a place that recently had severe weather. Write a newspaper article about the events.	Listen to daily weather reports for one week. Record as many weather words as you can. Create a collage to express the feelings of those words.	You learned about different types of lightning. Research and create a graphic organizer to show other types of weather, like rain, clouds, or storms.

Further Reading

 For more projects visit *LongmanCornerstone.com.*

The Amazing Universe, Paul Shipton
This Penguin Young Reader® is full of fantastic facts about the planets and our solar system.

Thunder Cake, Patricia Polacco
A storm is approaching and Katie is afraid. Her grandmother asks her to help bake a "thunder cake." As Katie dashes around gathering the things she needs, she forgets her fear of thunder. The cake is ready to eat before the storm is over.

71–72

Listening and Speaking Workshop

Give a How-to Presentation

You are going to write and give a how-to presentation. Then you will listen as your classmates give their presentations.

❶ Prepare

A. Choose a dangerous situation or a sports activity. You will present how to stay safe or prepare for it. Then your classmates will ask you questions. You can use formal or informal language in your presentation.

B. Think about the different steps. Decide on the sequence. Now write your how-to presentation. Remember to describe what you're going to demonstrate and then explain each step. Find props to use.

I am going to describe how to prepare for a blizzard. It is important to do these things before the snow arrives.

First make sure you have food that does not need to be cooked. Peanut butter and bread are good. Also you will need plenty of bottled water to drink. Next make sure the batteries in your flashlights and radios work. Then find out if you have extra blankets.

Second make a list of the things you need to buy.

Third go to the store and buy the things you need.

---

❷ Practice

Find a partner. Practice your presentation in front of your partner. Your partner will act out or mime your instructions. Work with your partner to improve your presentation. Switch roles.

❸ Present

As you speak, do the following:
- Speak clearly and slowly.
- Use your props while you speak.
- After your presentation, answer questions your classmates ask.

As you listen, do the following:
- Think about what you already know.
- Take notes.
- Think of questions to ask the speaker after the presentation.

❹ Evaluate

After you speak, answer these questions:
- ✔ Did you describe what you demonstrated?
- ✔ Did you explain each step?

After you listen, answer these questions:
- ✔ Did you take notes?
- ✔ Did you ask any questions?
- ✔ What was the how-to presentation about?

Retell it to a partner.
- ✔ Did the speaker use formal or informal language?
- ✔ Think about the general meaning of the demonstration. Can you think of a title for it? Tell your idea to the class.

Speaking Skills

A presentation can use formal or informal language. Choose which to use based on the purpose of the presentation and its audience.

Listening Skills

Be an active listener. Listen carefully to the spoken words. Watch for gestures and visuals.

Writing Workshop

Write a How-to Essay

Ongoing Writing Skills Practice

Writing Prompt

Write an essay explaining a process or how to do something. Present the steps of the process in order from first to last. To make the order clear, use words such as *first*, *next*, and *finally*.

❶ Prewrite G.O. 144

Review the writing you have done in this unit. Now choose a topic. Think about things you know how to do, such as downloading a song from the Internet or making popcorn. List the steps of the process in a graphic organizer like the one below.

A student named Andy listed his ideas like this:

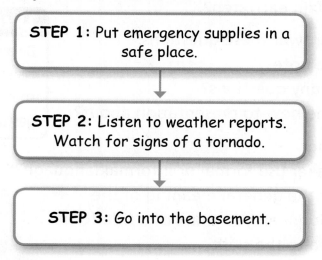

STEP 1: Put emergency supplies in a safe place.

STEP 2: Listen to weather reports. Watch for signs of a tornado.

STEP 3: Go into the basement.

❷ Draft

Use your graphic organizer to write a draft.
- Keep your purpose in mind—to explain how to do something.
- Present the steps in time order.

❸ Revise

Read your draft. Look for places where the writing needs improvement. Use the Writing Checklist to help you. Then revise your draft.

Here is how Andy revised his essay.

Six Traits of Writing Checklist

✔ **Ideas**
Did I explain the steps clearly?

✔ **Organization**
Are the steps in time order?

✔ **Voice**
Does my writing sound like me?

✔ **Word Choice**
Did I choose precise words?

✔ **Sentence Fluency**
Did I vary my sentence patterns?

✔ **Conventions**
Do my pronouns agree?

Andy Wong

Tornado Safety

You need to prepare for tornadoes before they hit. Tornadoes are powerful storms with fast winds. They can strike with little warning. They can destroy property and kill people. Here are things you can do to stay safe.

> **Revised** to make the meaning clearer.

First, gather emergency supplies and put them in a safe place. Choose a spot that is protected from the tornado s' winds. Include water, canned foods, a first-aid kit, a radio, a flash light, and batteries.

> **Revised** to correct spelling errors.

Then listen to reports if a tornado is predicted and watch for signs of it coming. A tornado looks like a funnel. Sometimes you can hear it coming. A tornado sounds like a waterfall.

> **Revised** to make the meaning clearer.

Finally ~~Next~~, if a tornado is on its way, go into the basement. Stay away from windows. Lie down and cover your head with your hands.

> **Revised** to choose a more effective transition word.

Tornadoes move fast. so You need to be prepared in order to stay safe.

> **Revised** to combine sentences.

❹ Edit

Check your work for errors. Trade papers with a partner. Use the Peer Review Checklist to give each other feedback. Edit your final draft in response to feedback from your partner and your teacher.

❺ Publish

Make a clean copy of your final draft. Share your essay with the class.

73–74

Peer Review Checklist

✓ The steps are clear.

✓ The steps in the correct order.

✓ All the information related to the topic

SPELLING TIP

The letters *gh* are sometime silent as in **sigh**, **high**, an **light**. Notice words with silent *gh* and learn their spelling patterns.

Listen to the sentences. Pay attention Audio
to the groups of words. Read aloud.

1. A volcano erupted almost 2,000 years ago in Pompeii.

2. We can follow tips to stay safe during thunder and lightning storms.

3. A family vacationing at the beach must find shelter when a hurricane hits.

Work in pairs. Take turns reading the passage below aloud for one minute. Count the number of words you read.

Boom! Suddenly, the top of Mount Vesuvius blew off!	9
Now the mountain had a crater. The volcano was erupting.	19
Fire and huge black clouds rose into the sky. The ground	30
Was shaking. People ran from their homes.	37
Ash and smoke covered the sun. Daytime turned into	46
darkness. Lava poured down the mountain. Hot ash and rocks	56
fell from the sky.	60
The ash covered people's heads, faces, and bodies. It	69
burned their eyes. It filled their mouths as they called	79
for help. The air became very thick with ash and gases.	90
It was hard to breathe.	95
The ash piled higher and higher. Soon, it buried	104
the city.	106

With your partner, find the words that slowed you down.

- Practice saying each word and then say the sentence each word is in.

- Then take turns reading the text again. Count the number of words you read.

WB
75–76

Test Preparation

Taking Tests

You will often take tests that help show what you know. Follow these tips to improve your test-taking skills.

Coaching Corner

Answering Test Items for Revising and Editing

- Revising and Editing Tests often ask you to look for corrections and improvements that a writer should make.

- Before you read the written selection, preview the questions and answer choices.

- After reading the whole selection, go back and carefully reread the sentence mentioned in the question. Do you notice any mistakes in grammar or punctuation?

- Read each of the answer choices to yourself to see if one of them sounds better than the sentence in the selection. Choose the answer that does the most to improve the whole sentence.

- Remember that sometimes the sentence will not need any corrections or improvements.

Read the following test sample. Study the tips in the box.

77–78

Read the selection. Then answer the questions.

(1) It stopped raining in the Southwest in the summer of 1931. (2) Crops died. (3) There was nothing left to hold the dirt on the ground. (4) Then the dust storms begin. (5) This event was called the Dust Bowl, and it lasted for 10 years. (6) There was dust everywhere. (7) There was dust in the food and in the water. (8) It is hard for animals and people to breathe. (9) Sometimes there was so much dust in the air, people couldn't see the sun. (10) The sky become so dark, it looked like night during the day.

1 What is the BEST way to revise sentence 4?

A Then the dust storms end.

B Then the dust storms begun.

C Then the dust storms began.

D No revision is needed.

2 What revision, if any, is necessary in sentence 8?

F It was hard for animals and people to breathe.

G It were hard for animals and people to breathe.

H It are hard for animals and people to breathe.

J No revision is needed.

3 What change, if any, should be made in sentence 10?

A Change *looked* to **look.**

B Change *become* to **became.**

C Change *become* to **were.**

D Make no change.

Tips

✔ Read sentence 4 in the selection again. What action is described?

✔ Read each answer choice to yourself. Think about how to form past tense verbs.

✔ Sentence 10 contains an irregular verb. Is it used correctly?

Telling Tales

Everyone enjoys a good story. You will read two tales and a play. They are different genres, or types of literature. What stories do you like to tell or read?

Reading

1 | Pourquoi Tale

Why Mosquitoes Buzz in People's Ears

2 | Play

The Shoemakers and the Elves

3 | Tall Tale

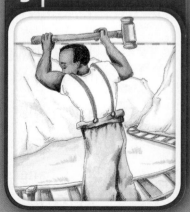

John Henry and the Machine

What do the characters in tales have in common?

Listening and Speaking

You will talk about telling tales. In the Listening and Speaking Workshop, you will perform a play.

Writing

You will practice narrative writing. In the Writing Workshop, you will write a story.

Quick Write

What is your favorite story?
Describe what happens.

DVD

VIEW AND RESPOND

Talk about the poster for this unit. Then watch and listen to the video and answer the questions at <u>LongmanCornerstone.com</u>.

What do you know about reading?

Words to Know

Listen and repeat. Use these words to talk about reading.

 a magazine

 a newspaper

 a recipe

 a cereal box

 a website

 directions

Practice

Work with a partner. Ask questions using the words above. Answer them using words from the box or your own ideas.

see photographs	get information	learn how to do something	see illustrations

Example: A: Why do you read a newspaper?

B: I read a newspaper to get information.

Write

Read the question. Write your answer in your notebook.

What do you like to read? Why?

Make Connections

Copy the sentences below into your notebook. Complete the sentences with the following words.

a cookbook

a computer

a board game

photographs

1. A ____ is fun to play with friends. Before we play, we always read the directions so we can learn the rules.

2. I like to go on ____ to get information. There are a lot of interesting websites that help me with my homework.

3. My mom loves to cook. She reads recipes from ____. She always measures the ingredients.

4. When I go to the dentist I like to read a magazine. There are many things to read and lots of ____ to look at.

What about you?

Talk with a partner. Talk about other things you can read.

Kids' Stories from around the World 🎧 Audio

Oklahoma, U.S.A.

Raymond

I live in Oklahoma. My father told me a tale about the first strawberries. He said they were made to help two friends who were angry with each other. When they shared the fruit, they became friends again. Now, I always share my strawberries.

David

I live in the United Kingdom. My house is near the National History Museum. I like to visit the fossil of a giant dinosaur. We call him Claws. My favorite poem is *Bones to Stones*. It is about a dinosaur just like Claws.

United Kingdom

Germany

Burkina Faso

Katya

I live in Germany. My favorite story is *Little Red-Cap*. In some countries, this story is called *Little Red Riding Hood*. The girl walks through the woods to visit her grandmother. She finds a surprise. A wolf is in her grandmother's bed!

Bacia

I am from Burkina Faso. The summers in Africa are hot and rainy. That means there are lots of mosquitoes. My grandmother tells a story about mosquitoes that buzz in people's ears.

What about you?

1. Do any of these stories sound familiar to you? Which ones?

2. Do you know of any stories or tales? Share them with the class.

What You Will Learn

Reading

- Vocabulary building: *Context, phonics*

- Reading strategy: *Identify events in a plot*

- Text type: *Literature (pourquoi tale)*

Grammar

Singular and plural nouns

Writing

Retell a familiar story

These words will help you understand the reading.

Key Words

tidbit

mischief

nonsense

duty

satisfied

council

Key Words

Why Mosquitoes Buzz in People's Ears is a pourquoi tale. It explains why mosquitoes can't talk.

Words in Context

1 Sasha and Pedro put a **tidbit** of food in the fish tank.

2 My little brother is always getting into **mischief**.

3 Jessie likes to whisper **nonsense** in Kevin's ear.

4 Every citizen has a **duty** to vote. Voting helps cities and towns make plans.

BALLOTS

5 Kelly was **satisfied** with the sandcastle she built.

6 This student **council** meets once a week. It is the school's government.

SANTA MONICA HIGH SCHOOL

Practice

Make flashcards to help you memorize the words.
- Write a word on the front.
- On the back, write a sentence, but leave a blank where the key word should be.

Make Connections

What are your duties at home? What is a student's duty at school? After discussing these questions, write your responses in your notebook using the key words.

WB

79

These words will help you talk about the reading.

Academic Words

emerge
appear or come out from somewhere

react
say or do something because of something else

respond
answer

Academic Words

Words in Context

In spring, many animals **emerge** from their winter homes.

People often **react** to a mosquito by waving it away.

Students should always **respond** politely when a teacher speaks to them.

Practice

Write the sentences in your notebook. Choose an academic word to complete each sentence.

1. Please _____ to the test question. Write your answer neatly.

2. The soccer fans _____ to a each goal with cheers.

3. Moths will _____ from their cocoons.

Apply

Ask and answer with partner.

1. How do you **react** when you do well on a test?

2. How do students **emerge** from their classroom on the last day of school?

3. How do you **respond** when a friend asks for a favor?

80

Phonics

Long Vowel Pairs

Long vowel sounds can be spelled with two vowels together
making a pair. Listen. Then read each word aloud.

Long Vowel Pairs				
Long *a*	Long *e*	Long *i*	Long *o*	Long *u*
wait, day	bean, tree	cried	roam, toes	true, fruit

Did you notice that each word has two vowels together?
Which vowel do you hear? Which vowel is silent?

Rule

When two vowels are together, the first vowel is usually long,
and the second vowel is silent.

w a i t   b e a n   t r u e

Practice

Work with a partner. Sound out the words in the box. Then
write the word that has the vowel sound.

road	skies	clue	fail	need

1. long *a* _____

2. long *e* _____

3. long *i* _____

4. long *o* _____

5. long *u* _____

81

More About

How are animal characters like people?

 Listen to the Audio.
Listen for the general meaning. Think about the situation or context. Use this to help you understand the story.

Reading Strategy

Identify Events in a Plot

A plot is made up of events from the story. Identifying the events can help you understand the story. As you read:

- Pay attention to the order in which events happen.

- Notice how one action leads to another action.

Listen as your teacher models the reading strategy.

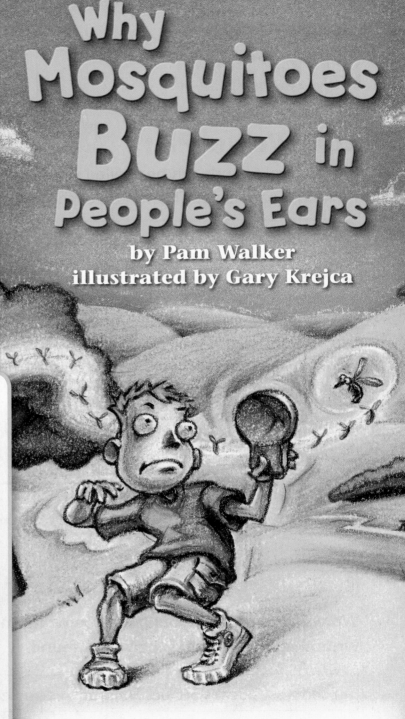

Why Mosquitoes Buzz in People's Ears

by Pam Walker
illustrated by Gary Krejca

Have you ever heard a mosquito buzzing in your ear? Here's where that insect's **annoying** habit came from.

---

annoying   making you feel a little angry

Reading Skill

Ask your classmates or teacher when you do not understand a word, phrase, or language structure.

One summer day, Mosquito saw Turtle sunbathing on a rock.

He flew over to his friend and whispered in her ear. "I have a tidbit of news!"

"You should not **gossip**," said Turtle.

"But wait until you hear this!" said Mosquito. "Farmer grew a carrot as large as an elephant!"

"That is nonsense!" Turtle cried. "I don't want to hear it!" She stuffed leaves in her ears and walked away.

Snake was in a tree branch when Turtle walked by.

"Hi, Turtle!" he hissed. "It'sssss me." But Turtle could not hear him.

---

gossip   talk about someone in a way that is not nice

Before You Go On   Why didn't the turtle **respond** to the snake?

"Turtle must be mad at me," Snake thought sadly. He **slithered** out of the tree to hide under a log. Mouse lived in the log. When she saw Snake coming, she ran from her home.

"What's wrong?" Rabbit asked the **timid** mouse.

"I have no time to talk," said Mouse. "Run! Danger!"

So Rabbit ran as fast as she could. "Run!" she cried. "Danger!"

Monkey heard Rabbit's cries. "Something bad is happening!" he thought. "It is my duty to tell the others!"

He jumped from tree to tree. "Run!" he called. "Danger!"

---

slithered   moved by sliding along the ground

timid   shy or scared

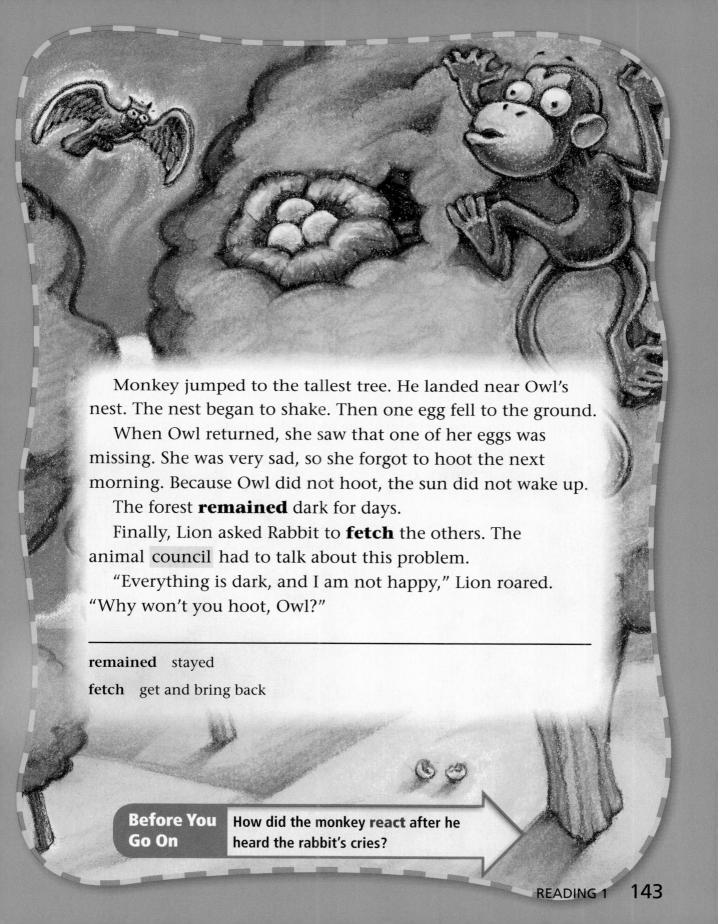

Monkey jumped to the tallest tree. He landed near Owl's nest. The nest began to shake. Then one egg fell to the ground.

When Owl returned, she saw that one of her eggs was missing. She was very sad, so she forgot to hoot the next morning. Because Owl did not hoot, the sun did not wake up.

The forest **remained** dark for days.

Finally, Lion asked Rabbit to **fetch** the others. The animal council had to talk about this problem.

"Everything is dark, and I am not happy," Lion roared. "Why won't you hoot, Owl?"

---

remained stayed

fetch get and bring back

Before You Go On How did the monkey **react** after he heard the rabbit's cries?

"I am too sad to hoot," said Owl. "Monkey broke one of my eggs!"

Lion looked at Monkey. "Rabbit said there was danger!" said Monkey. "I wanted to **warn** everyone!"

Lion looked at Rabbit. "Mouse told me to run!" Rabbit said.

Lion looked at Mouse. "Snake came to my house! I was afraid he would eat me!" cried Mouse.

"I wassss not hungry. I was sssssad," hissed Snake. "Turtle would not ssssspeak to me."

Just then, Turtle walked by.

"Turtle!" Lion roared. "Are you Snake's friend?"

"What?" Turtle removed the leaves from her ears. "Yes, I am Snake's friend."

---

warn   tell someone that something bad or dangerous may happen

"Then why didn't you speak when Snake said hello?" asked Lion.

"I did not hear him," said Turtle. "Mosquito gossips, so I put leaves in my ears."

"All this mischief started with you, Mosquito," the angry lion said. "You may never talk again."

All the animals were satisfied, but not Mosquito. Even today mosquitoes want to talk. But all they can do is buzzzzz!

W B
82–84

Reading Strategy

Identify Events in a Plot

- What action started the events of the story?

- Did identifying the events in the plot help you understand the story? How?

Think It Over

1. **Recall**   Who decides that the animal council must meet?

2. **Comprehend**   How does Mouse **react** when she sees the snake?

3. **Analyze**   Does the true story finally **emerge**? Explain.

Learning Strategies

Sequence of Events

In many stories, events happen in a certain order. That order is called the **sequence**.

 **Practice**

Read these events from *Why Mosquitoes Buzz in People's Ears*. List them in order.

- Turtle told Mosquito that Mosquito should not gossip.
- Turtle stuffed leaves in her ears and walked away.
- Mosquito flew over to tell Turtle a tidbit of news.
- Mosquito whispered some gossip in Turtle's ear anyway.
- Mosquito saw Turtle sunbathing on a rock.

Use a Sequence of Events Chart

A Sequence of Events Chart helps you put events in the correct order. Start with the first event. Then write each event that happens after that. Finish with the last event.

Copy and complete this chart.

- Reread the story. List the tale's events in the correct order.
- Share your chart with a partner.
- Discuss what would happen if someone read the events in the wrong order.

Sequence of Events in *Why Mosquitoes Buzz in People's Ears*	
First	Mosquito sees Turtle sunbathing.
Next	
Next	
Next	Owl forgets to hoot.
Next	
Next	
Last	Lion tells Mosquito he can never talk again.

85

Apply

Using the pictures in the reading, retell the story to a partner. Use some of the key words.

Extension

Utilize Do you know how to play Telephone? Form a circle with your classmates. The first person whispers a sentence to the next person. That person whispers the same sentence to the next person. The last person says the sentence aloud. Did the message change? How?

Grammar

Singular and Plural Nouns

A **noun** is a person, place, or thing. Use a **singular noun** for one item.
Use **plural nouns** for more than one item.

Singular	Plural
a cat	three cats

Review the spelling rules for making plural nouns.

For most nouns, add -*s*	turtle ⟶ turtle**s**
For nouns ending in -*ch*, -*sh*, -*ss*, or -*x*, add -*es*	bran**ch** ⟶ bran**ches**
For nouns ending in consonant + -*y*, change the -*y* to -*ies*	ba**by** ⟶ bab**ies**
For nouns ending in vowel + -*y*, add -*s*	da**y** ⟶ day**s**
For most nouns ending in consonant + *o*, add -*es*	mosquit**o** ⟶ mosquito**es**
For most nouns ending in vowel + *o*, add -*s*	stud**io** ⟶ studio**s**
For most nouns ending in -*f* or -*fe*, change the -*f* or -*fe* to -*ves*	lea**f** ⟶ lea**ves**
	kni**fe** ⟶ kni**ves**

Irregular plural nouns change in form.

child ⟶ children	person ⟶ people	mouse ⟶ mice

Remember subject-verb agreement with singular and plural nouns in sentences.

	Noun	Verb
Singular Subject	This dog	run**s** fast.
Plural Subject	These dogs	**run** fast.

Change each singular noun to plural. Make
any changes necessary to correct subject-verb
agreement. Write the sentences.

Example: The flower blooms in the summer.

1. The child is getting into mischief.

2. The country has beautiful beaches.

3. The man **responds** to the fire alarm.

4. The wolf **emerges** in the evening.

5. The mouse **reacts** whenever a cat is near.

Apply

Work with a partner. Choose a noun from the list below. Say
whether it's singular or plural, and use it in a sentence. Then
your partner will change it to its opposite form and use it in
a sentence.

Example: A: Brushes is plural. That store sells many brushes.
B: Brush is singular. My dog chewed his brush.

brushes	person
hero	knife
council	women
cries	duty
shelves	essay
lunch	habit

86

Grammar Check ✓

How do you form the plural for
most nouns ending in -f or -fe?

Writing

Ongoing Writing Skills Practice

Retell a Familiar Story

When you retell a story, you explain what happened in your own words. Ask yourself: Did I retell the most important events or actions? Did I retell the events in the correct order? Did I use my own words?

Writing Prompt

Write a paragraph that retells or narrates a familiar story from a book that you enjoy. Be sure to use singular and plural nouns correctly.

❶ Prewrite G.O. 144

Choose a familiar story to retell. Think about what happened in the beginning, middle, and end of the story. List these events in a sequence of events chart.

A student named Josh listed his ideas in this sequence of events chart:

❷ Draft

Beginning
A crow sat in a tree with a piece of cheese in its beak. A hungry fox walked by. The crow flew higher.

Middle
The crow did not like foxes so she flew to a very high branch. The fox told the crow she was the most beautiful crow of all. Could she sing too?

End
When the crow opened her beak to sing, she dropped the cheese. The fox ate it.

Use your sequence of events chart to help you write a first draft.

- Keep in mind your purpose for writing—to retell.
- In your own words retell the events from the beginning, middle, and end of the story in order.

❸ Revise

Read over your draft. Look for places where the story events are out of order. Use the Writing Checklist to help you identify problems. Then revise your draft.

❹ Edit

Check your work for errors. Trade papers with a partner to get feedback. Use the Peer Review Checklist on page 402. Edit your final draft.

❺ Publish

Prepare a clean copy of your final draft. Share your paragraph with the class. Save your work. You will need to refer to it in the Writing Workshop.

Here is Josh's story:

Writing Checklist

Ideas

✓ I told the events from the beginning, middle, and end of the story.

✓ I used my own words.

Conventions

✓ I used singular and plural nouns correctly.

✓ My pronouns and verbs agree.

Josh Snyder

The Fox and The Crow

One morning a black crow sat in a tree with many branches. The crow held a piece of cheese in its beak. Soon a fox walked by. The hungry fox loved cheese. But the crow did not like foxes, so she flew to a very high tree branch. The smart fox called up to the crow. He said she was more beautiful than any of the other crows. But could she sing too? Now the proud crow was also a show-off. She opened her beak very wide and sang for the fox. Of course the cheese fell straight down and the fox ate it.

87–88

What You Will Learn

Reading

- Vocabulary building: *Context, phonics*

- Reading strategy: *Make inferences*

- Text type: *Literature (play)*

Grammar
Possessives

Writing
Write a letter to a friend or family member

These words will help you understand the reading.

Key Words

fine

whisk

stitches

stroke

bare

wink

Key Words

The Shoemakers and the Elves is a play about two elves and two shoemakers who help each other.

Words in Context

1 The queen wore her **fine** clothing when her picture was painted.

2 Taxis quickly **whisk** riders across town.

3 Many red **stitches** hold this baseball together.

4 At the stroke of midnight,
Cinderella ran out of the palace.

5 Old Mother Hubbard's cupboard
was bare . There was no food inside.

6 How much time does it
take you to wink an eye?

Practice

Make flashcards to help you memorize the words.
- Write a word on the front.
- On the back, write a sentence, but leave a blank where the key
  word should be.

Make Connections

"As quick as a wink" means "very quickly." People use that expression
even when something does not happen as quickly as a wink. What are
some expressions you use? Explain what they mean.

WB
89

These words will help you talk about the reading.

Academic Words

appreciate
be thankful or grateful for something

benefit
provide something helpful or good

infer
form an opinion based on information you have

90

Academic Words

Words in Context

The students **appreciate** the teacher's help.

Doing your chores will **benefit** the whole family because your home will stay tidy.

Mom could **infer** that Leo was home because she saw his backpack by the door.

Practice

Write the sentences in your notebook. Use an academic word in each sentence.

1. They _____ everything the coach does for them.

2. When you read a story try to _____ how the characters get along.

3. All the students will _____ from the new computers in the classroom.

Apply

Ask and answer with a partner.

1. How do you show that you **appreciate** your friend's help?

2. How does your homework **benefit** you?

3. How could people **infer** that you like to help others?

Phonics

Vowel Pair: *ea*

Each word below has the vowel pair *ea*. Listen to your teacher.
Then read each word aloud.

Vowel Pair *ea*	
Long e	**Short e**
eat	bread
each	head
speak	ready

Rule

The vowel pair *ea* can have two sounds: the long e sound,
as in **eat,** or the short e sound, as in **bread**. If you see a word you do
not know, try saying the *ea* sound both ways.

Practice

Read the sentences with a partner. Take turns.

- They will sneak into the house.
- The mice will eat cheese instead of bread.
- Their shoes are made from leather.
- The girl thinks she is dreaming.

1. List the words in which *ea* has the long e sound.

2. Then list the words in which *ea* has the short e sound.

LITERATURE

Play

More About

Why do tales often tell about characters that help each other?

 Listen to the Audio.
Listen for the general meaning. Think about the situation or context. Use this to help you understand the story.

Reading Strategy

Make Inferences

When you make inferences, you are figuring out what the author means but doesn't say.

- Think about what you already know that the text doesn't tell you.

- Use the information in the text and your own experiences.

Listen as your teacher models the reading strategy.

The Shoemakers and the Elves

by Amanda Hong
illustrated by Sheila Bailey

Cast

Pixie, a female elf
Lumkin, a male elf
Amelia, a shoemaker and Diego's wife
Diego, a shoemaker and Amelia's husband

Scene 1: Two elves are looking into the window of a house. Two **elderly** shoemakers are inside. They are yawning. The elves wear **tattered** clothing. They are cold.

Lumkin: Let's play a trick on them!

Pixie: No, Lumkin. I think we have had enough fun for one day. We need a warm place to rest.

Lumkin: You're right. I don't want to get chased out of another house. I'm cold.

Pixie: [She looks in the window again.] Those people look tired.

Lumkin: And their shelves look bare. The shoemakers have nothing to sell.

Pixie: They're talking. Let's listen.

---

elderly   old

tattered   old and torn

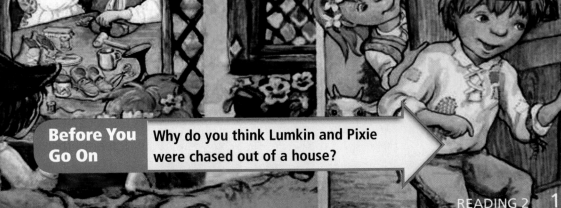

Before You Go On   Why do you think Lumkin and Pixie were chased out of a house?

[The shoemakers are tired and worried. Tools for tomorrow's work are on a table.]

Diego: I don't know how we can survive. We have no more leather to make shoes.

Amelia: What will we do?

Diego: Maybe we should close our shop.

Amelia: Then what will we do? Sell firewood?

Diego: Why not? I can chop down the walls to find wood.

[They yawn as they walk upstairs.]

Amelia: Let's sleep. We'll think about this tomorrow.

[The elves enter the shoemakers' shop.]

Pixie: This is sad, Lumkin.

Reading Skill

As you read, use the pictures to help you understand the words and ideas.

Lumkin: Yes, I am very sad. There is no bread here for us to eat.

Pixie: I think the shoemakers' problems are bigger than ours. We should help these people.

Lumkin: He wants firewood. Let's chop up the house!

Pixie: No tricks, Lumkin.

Lumkin: We could finish making the shoes. Then tomorrow the shoemakers will get a big surprise.

Pixie: Yes! We will make so many beautiful shoes. Everyone will want to buy them.

Lumkin: If you get that cheese on the **mousetrap**, I will make the shoes as quick as a wink.

Pixie: You always ask me to do the hard things.

---

mousetrap   trap that uses food to catch mice

Before You Go On   What could you **infer** about Lumkin wanting the cheese?

[The elves finish working.]

Lumkin: Let's put away the tools and leather.

Pixie: Whisk the mess away. Let's go play!

[The elves leave. The next morning, the shoemakers come downstairs. They find the new shoes. They are **speechless**.]

Amelia: Look, Diego! Shoes! I must be dreaming!

Diego: Did you get up and work last night?

Amelia: No! I was going to ask you the same thing!

Diego: Then I must be dreaming, too! These shoes are beautiful.

Amelia: Look at these stitches! The **quality** is very fine.

Diego: Even we could not have made such special shoes.

Amelia: Let's put them in the window.

[They embrace.]

---

speechless   unable to speak

quality   degree to which something is good or bad

[One week later, the shoemakers sit at the table.]

Diego: We are very lucky. Every night, someone makes shoes for us.

Amelia: And every day, we sell all those new shoes. We have so many **customers** now.

Diego: Who do you think is making the shoes, Amelia?

Amelia: I have no idea, Diego. But I would like to thank them. Wouldn't you?

Diego: Yes. But how?

Amelia: I have an idea!

[That night, Diego and Amelia do not go to bed. Instead, they hide behind a curtain. At the stroke of midnight, the two elves appear at the window.]

Diego: [whispering] Elves?

Amelia: [whispering] Elves! How **delightful**!

---

customers   people who buy goods and services

delightful   very nice

Before You Go On How do the shoemakers show that they **appreciate** the new shoes?

[The clock rings twelve times. Lumkin and Pixie **sneak** into the house through the window.]

Pixie: Try to be quiet, Lumkin. We do not want to wake up the people.

[Lumkin runs to the mousetrap. He grabs the **bait** and eats it.]

Pixie: That cheese is for mice.

Lumkin: It's for hungry elves, too. I like to eat before I work.

Pixie: Well, there is a lot of work to do tonight.

[The elves go to the table and begin working. The shoemakers watch from behind the curtain.]

Amelia: We should do something nice for those hard workers.

Diego: I have an idea!

---

sneak   go somewhere very quietly so as not to be seen or heard

bait   food that is used to attract and catch animals

[The next night, the shoemakers put two packages on the table. Then they hide and **peek** through the curtains.]

Lumkin: It's midnight.

Pixie: That means it's time to go to work.

[The elves look around. The table is bare except for the gifts.]

Lumkin: Where is the leather? Where are the tools?

Pixie: What is this?

[The elves open the packages.]

Pixie: These beautiful things are for us!

[They try on the clothes and shoes. Then they dance with joy.]

Lumkin: Let's go outside and play!

Pixie: But what about our work?

Lumkin and Pixie: Ha ha!

[The elves laugh as they dance. The shoemakers smile as the happy elves leave.]

---

peek   look secretly at something that you are not supposed to see

92–94

Reading Strategy

Make Inferences

- What time did the elves come?
- How can you make that inference?

Think It Over

1. **Recall**   What problem do Amelia and Diego have?

2. **Comprehend**   Do the elves **appreciate** the gifts from the shoemakers? How do they show it?

3. **Analyze**   How do the elves and the shoemakers both **benefit** in this story?

Learning Strategies

Infer and Predict

To **infer** is to figure out something that the author doesn't directly tell you. To **predict** is to make guesses about what will happen.

Practice

Make inferences or predictions about the passage.

> The manager hired Manuel instead of Joe. He needed an experienced waiter, and he did not have time to teach Joe everything. Joe hoped to find a job soon. Summer vacation had already started. School would begin again in September. There were lots of "Help Wanted" signs on Main Street. Joe would keep looking for a job.

1. Has Joe been a waiter before?
2. Has Manuel been a waiter before?
3. Is Joe a student?
4. Will Joe return to school soon?
5. Does Joe want a job?
6. Will Joe get a job?

Use an Infer and Predict Chart

An Infer and Predict Chart helps you answer questions about a story or play.

Work with a partner. Read the dialogue in the first column.

- Discuss what you know about the elves and the shoemakers.
- Answer the questions in the second column.

Dialogue	Infer/Predict
Lumkin: Let's play a trick on them! **Pixie:** No, Lumkin. I think we have had enough fun for one day. **Lumkin:** You're right. I don't want to get chased out of another house. I'm cold.	**1. Infer:** Which elf seems more sensible? **2. Infer:** Have the elves been chased out of a house before?
Lumkin: If you get that cheese on the mousetrap, I will make the shoes as quick as a wink. **Pixie:** You always ask me to do the hard things.	**3. Predict:** What will Lumkin and Pixie do with the cheese? **4. Infer:** Which does Pixie think is harder, getting cheese or making shoes?
Pixie: These beautiful things are for us! **Lumkin:** Let's go outside and play! **Pixie:** But what about our work? **Lumkin and Pixie:** Ha ha!	**5. Infer:** Do the elves like their gifts? **6. Predict:** Will Lumkin and Pixie come back to work after they play?

Summarize the story to a partner.
Use some key words.

Extension

95

Utilize Think of a chore you can do. Explain it to a partner. Ask your partner to repeat the directions. Then switch roles and follow your partner's directions.

Grammar

Possessives

Use a **possessive** to show that someone or something "possesses," or owns, something. To form a possessive with singular or plural nouns that don't end in -s, we add 's (apostrophe s).

Singular Noun	Object	Plural Noun	Object
The girl's	dress	The children's	books
The group's	notes	The women's	team

To form the possessive of plural nouns that end in -s, we add an apostrophe (') to the end of the word.

Plural Noun	Object
The students'	school
The Raines'	house

For two subjects that both own something, only the second one takes an 's.

Compound Noun	Object	Meaning
Miguel and Wanda's	dog	*The dog belongs to both Miguel and Wanda.*

Possessive pronouns show possession, too. They do not take an 's.

Possessive Pronoun	Object
My, your, his, her, its, our, their	cats

Practice

Change each phrase to make the nouns show possession. Write the sentences.

Example: The clothing of the elves

The elves' clothing.

1. The shoes belonging to customers

2. The  of the shoe

3. The horses belonging to Diego

4. The problems of the shoemakers

5. The dance of Lumkin and Pixie

Apply

Work with a partner. Ask and answer the questions about *The Shoemaker and the Elves.* If you need to, look back at the reading. Use possessive nouns in your answers.

Example: A: Who is Amelia?

B: She's a shoemaker. She's Diego's wife.

- Who is Amelia?
- Who is Diego?
- Whose shelves are bare?
- What is Pixie and Lumkin's problem?
- Whose problems are bigger? Why?
- Whose cheese does Lumkin eat?
- Whose packages are on the table?

96

Grammar Check ✓

Why do we add 's to nouns?

Writing

Ongoing Writing Skills Practice

Write a Friendly Letter

In a friendly letter, you share your experiences A friendly letter includes these parts: date, greeting, body, closing, and signature.

Writing Prompt

Write a friendly letter about an interesting event. You can write to a friend or to someone in your family. Be sure to use possessives correctly.

❶ Prewrite

Choose an event to write about. The event can take place in your school, home, or community. List your ideas in a graphic organizer.

A student named Kate used this graphic organizer:

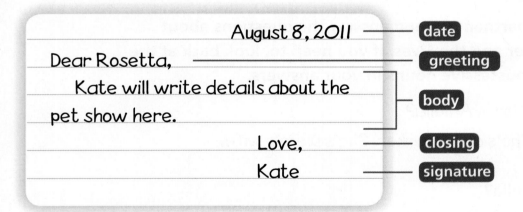

❷ Draft

Use your graphic organizer to help you write a first draft.
* Keep in mind your purpose for writing—to write a letter.
* Write information in each part of the letter and include interesting details.

❸ Revise

Read over your draft. Look for places where the writing needs improvement. Use the Writing Checklist to help you identify problems. Then revise your draft.

❹ Edit

Check your work for errors. Trade papers with a partner to get feedback. Use the Peer Review Checklist on page 402.

❺ Publish

Prepare a clean copy of your final draft. Share your paragraph with the class. Save your work. You will need to refer to it in the Writing Workshop.

Writing Checklist

Ideas

✔ I filled in all the parts of a friendly letter.

Word Choice

✔ I included interesting details.

Conventions

✔ I used possessives correctly.

Here is Kate's personal letter:

32 First Avenue
Philadelphia, PA
August 8, 2011

Dear Rosetta,

　　Last Saturday my dog Sam was in a neighborhood pet show at Logan Park. Many of our neighbors' pets were in the show, too. People brought their dogs, cats, rabbits, birds, and fish. I didn't think most of the animals would get along. But they did, most of the time! Then, in the middle of a contest, Sam's collar fell off and he raced around the park. I guess he won't win prizes for being well behaved. It didn't matter. It was a wonderful day! Write soon.

Love,

Kate

WB
97–98

What You Will Learn

Reading

- Vocabulary building: *Context, word study*
- Reading strategy: *Identify characters*
- Text type: *Literature (tall tale)*

Grammar
Quotations

Writing
Write a dialogue between two characters

These words will help you understand the reading.

Key Words

mighty

sledgehammer

machine

boasted

sputter

Key Words

John Henry and the Machine is about a contest between a man and a machine.

Words in Context

❶ An elephant is a mighty animal that can help people move large objects.

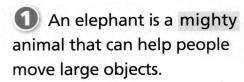

❷ A person can use a sledgehammer to break up rocks.

❸ A machine can help people work or get from place to place, but they can break down if you don't take care of them.

④ The boy **boasted** that he was faster than his brother.

⑤ A car will **sputter** when it runs out of gas.

Practice

Add a page to your vocabulary notebook.

- Divide your page into three columns: the new words, their definitions, and drawings of the words when possible.

- Test yourself by covering one of the columns.

Make Connections

Machines can't do everything that people can do. What is something you can do that a machine cannot? Draw a picture to show one of the skills you are good at. Then write a caption under your picture. Present your drawing and read your caption to the class.

These words will help you
talk about the reading.

Academic Words

anticipate
guess or expect
that something
will happen

display
show

scenario
setting or situation

Academic Words

Words in Context

We did not **anticipate** the storm—it was a
big surprise.

The collectors **display** their coins in a glass case
for all to see.

One possible **scenario** for the plot of our play
could be a girl looking for her lost dog.

Practice

**Write the sentences in your notebook. Choose an
academic word to complete each sentence.**

1. We ＿＿＿ good judgment when we think
   carefully before we act.

2. This is a very familiar story. I can ＿＿＿ the end
   of this story before it happens.

3. Here is the ＿＿＿: the crime happens at night in
   an old building.

Apply

Ask and answer with a partner.

1. What is one thing that happened recently that
   you did not **anticipate**?

2. How would you **display** your favorite toy?

3. Can you imagine a **scenario** in which
   something surprising might happen? Describe it.

Word Study

Synonyms and Antonyms

Notice the words in red. What do they mean?

> The horse ran like the wind. It had powerful legs that were so strong.

The words **powerful** and **strong** both mean "having great power or strength." They are synonyms. **Synonyms** are words that mean the same or almost the same thing.

The word **weak** means "not having strength or power." **Weak** and **strong** are antonyms. **Antonyms** are words that have opposite meanings.

Practice

Work with a partner. Replace each underlined word with a synonym or an antonym from the box.

1. I'd love to <u>chat</u> some more.

2. The horse was <u>weak</u>.

3. Where did you <u>wander</u>?

4. Can we finish our work <u>now</u>?

later	roam
strong	talk

LITERATURE

Tall Tale

THE BIG QUESTION

More About

How is John Henry similar to characters in other tall tales?

Audio **Listen to the Audio.**
Listen for the general meaning. Think about the situation or context. Use the pictures to help you understand the selection.

Reading Strategy

Identify Characters

Characters are the people or animals in a story or poem. The main characters are the most important ones. The minor characters are less important. Think of a fairy tale you know well (for example, *Cinderella*). Then answer these questions:

- Who are the characters?
- Who is the main character? (There could be more than one in a story.)
- Who are the minor characters?

Listen as your teacher models the reading strategy.

John Henry and the Machine

by Michael Dunn Moriarty
illustrated by Nicole Laizure

The world is full of stories about the mighty John Henry. But he started out as a baby, just like the rest of us. The only difference was that even as a baby, John Henry could lift a sledgehammer over his head.

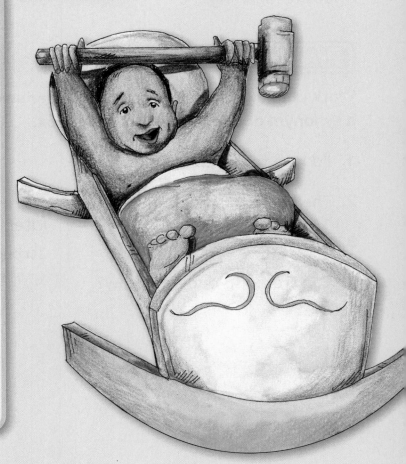

Young John Henry loved that big hammer. He liked to **pound** on rocks. Up went the hammer, and then down it came. John Henry could turn big rocks into dust.

When he grew up, John Henry worked for the railroad. He was bigger and stronger than everybody else on the job. All day long, he hammered steel **spikes** into rocks. He broke every rock that was in the way of the railroad.

John Henry was as happy as a man could be. Then a stranger brought a new machine to town.

---

pound   to hit very hard

spikes   pointed metal objects that can be hammered into rocks to break them apart

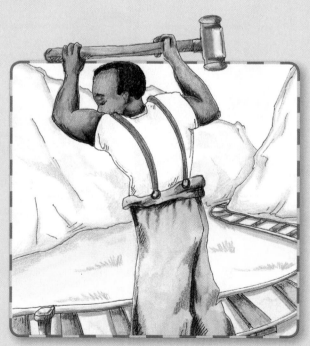

Before You Go On   What do you think the stranger's machine can do?

The stranger boasted that his **drilling** machine could do more work than ten men.

"Impossible!" John Henry cried. "No machine can do more work than I can."

The stranger challenged John Henry to a contest. He wanted to prove what his machine could do.

He pointed to a wall of rock. "Let's see who can drill through that!" Then he started his machine. John Henry raised his hammer.

John Henry and the machine worked. They worked all day and all night. They each broke through the thick wall, one rock at a time.

---

drilling   creating a hole in something, usually with a pointed object

The next morning, dust and people were everywhere. A crowd had gathered to watch the contest. They came to cheer for John Henry.

By noon, the stranger's machine began to sputter. But John Henry was still going strong.

Suddenly, the machine hissed. Then it died. John Henry brought his hammer down for one final blow.

When the dust cleared, everyone saw that John Henry had broken through the rock wall!

"You won the contest!" they cried.

John Henry smiled. "Yes, I did," he said. "Now, I just want to get back to work."

102–104

Reading Strategy

Identify Characters

- Who were the characters in the story?
- Who was the main character? If there was more than one, who were they?
- Who was a minor character? If there was more than one, who were they?

Think It Over

1. **Recall** What was the **scenario** that led someone to suggest a race?

2. **Analyze** Why did the stranger **anticipate** that his machine would win?

3. **Comprehend** What feeling in John Henry does the illustration on this page **display**?

American Tall Tale Characters

▲ Paul Bunyan

Paul Bunyan was a giant lumberjack with some unusual skills. Legend has it that he could cut down an entire forest with one swing of his axe. Stories of Paul Bunyan's adventures almost always include his giant blue ox named Babe.

▲ Johnny Appleseed

Johnny Appleseed is a legendary character based on a real American pioneer named John Chapman, who lived from 1774 to 1845. Johnny planted trees and gave away apple seeds as he journeyed west. He lived a simple life, walked great distances, and wore a cooking pot on his head as a hat.

▲ John Henry

John Henry was probably based on a real man. John Henry may have been a slave born in the 1840s. He was the most famous and strongest steel-driver who worked for the Chesapeake and Ohio Railroad. He raced a steam-powered drill through a stone mountain and won.

▲ Sally Ann Thunder

Sally Ann Thunder was the legendary wife of Davy Crockett. She was a fearless woman who scared a grizzly bear out of a cove and tossed an alligator many miles.

Activity to Do

These illustrations use pictures and words to tell about famous characters from American Tall Tales.

- Research one of these characters that interests you.

- Create two pages, using pictures and words, to tell about that character.

Learning Strategies

Identify Character

Characters are the people or animals in a story or poem.
The main characters are the most important ones. The minor
characters are less important.

Practice

**Make a list of all the characters you can remember from each
of these fairy tales. On each list, circle the main character.**

1. Cinderella
2. Little Red Riding Hood
3. Goldilocks and the Three Bears
4. The Three Little Pigs

Use a Character Web

A Character Web can help you organize information about characters in a story or poem.

 G.O. 154

Copy this Character Web. Use it to show what you know about John Henry.

- Complete your web with information from the story.
- Share your web with a partner.
- Discuss why it is important to know more about a main character.

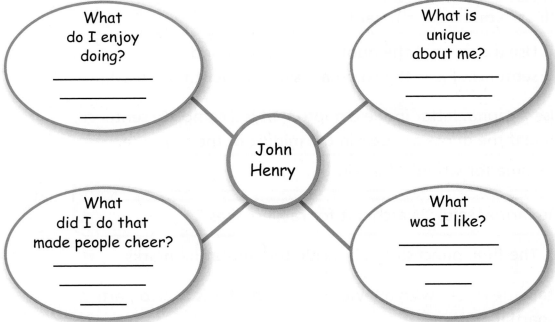

What
do I enjoy
doing?
_____
_____
_____

What is
unique
about me?
_____
_____
_____

John
Henry

What
did I do that
made people cheer?
_____
_____
_____

What
was I like?
_____
_____
_____

**Retell the story to a partner.
You can refer to the pictures
as you speak.**

Extension

 105

Utilize Talk with your partner about another story that has a character who wins a contest. Work together to write and draw a comic strip of the character and the adventure. Share and **display** your comic strip to the class.

Grammar

Quotations

Quotation marks show the exact words that a person said or wrote. Place quotation marks next to the quoted letters, with no extra space. Always set off a quote with a comma. Follow these rules for quotation marks.

1. Always use quotation marks in pairs: one pair at the beginning and one pair at the end of the quoted words.

    "I'll call you back," she said.

    - Use a comma if the quote ends in the middle of a sentence. Place the comma inside the quotation marks.

2. Use a capital letter inside a quote that is a complete sentence, even if the quote appears in the middle of the sentence.

    "It's time for school," he said.

    The farmer said, "Watch out for rattlesnakes."

    - The final punctuation is inside the quotation marks.

3. Start the quote with a lower-case letter if it is in two parts or a partial quote.

    "Whatever you do," said the coach, "don't look down."
    They said the moon is "a big, holey circle of Swiss cheese."

4. Use quotation marks to set off titles of short stories, poems, songs, and articles.

    Have you read the poem "Where the Sidewalk Ends"?

    - Question marks go outside when the title isn't a question.

Practice

Rewrite the sentences using quotation marks.

Example: Impossible! John Henry cried.
              "Impossible" John Henry cried.

1. My drilling machine can do more work than ten men, the stranger boasted .

2. The teacher asked What's the **scenario**?

3. John Henry said My sledgehammer and I can break through the wall faster than the machine.

4. The ant is small but mighty our teacher told us.

5. He said We don't **anticipate** any trouble.

Apply

Work with a partner. Ask and answer these questions about *John Henry and the Machine.* **Write down the answers using quotation marks correctly.**

Example: A: What did the infant John Henry lift over his head?

             B: "He lifted a sledgehammer over his head," the student said.

- What kind of machine did the stranger bring?
- Who won the contest?
- What did John Henry say after he won?
- What kind of sounds did the machine make?

106

Grammar Check ✓

What do we use quotation marks to show?

Writing

Write a Dialogue between Two Characters

Ongoing Writing Skills Practice

A **dialogue** is a conversation between two people. It tells their exact words. Always use quotations marks to set off what each speaker says.

Writing Prompt

Write a narrative paragraph that includes a dialogue between two make-believe characters, either people or animals. The characters should talk to each other about a special event. Be sure to use quotation marks correctly.

❶ Prewrite

G.O. 149

Think of two make-believe characters. These speakers will talk to each other about a special event. List the characters' names on the top of a T-chart. Under each name, write a few words or phrases that will be used in the dialogue.

A student named Rob listed his ideas in this T-chart:

❷ Draft

Use your T-chart to help you write a first draft.

- Keep in mind your purpose for writing—to write a dialogue.
- Remember to set off each speaker's exact words in quotation marks.

Maria

1. Maria liked exhibit of old toys in Children's Museum.
2. Dolls' faces were hand-painted.
3. Amazing to go back in time.

Henry

1. Henry liked toy exhibit too.
2. Some dolls over 150 years old.
3. Kids wore heavy shoes when they played ball.

---

❸ Revise

Read over your draft. Look for places where the dialogue needs improvement. Use the Writing Checklist to help you.

❹ Edit

Check your work for errors. Trade papers with a partner to get feedback. Use the Peer Review Checklist on page 402. Edit your final draft in response to feedback from your partner and your teacher.

❺ Publish

Prepare a clean copy of your final draft. Share your paragraph with the class. Save your work. You will need to refer to it in the Writing Workshop.

Here is Rob's dialogue:

Writing Checklist

Ideas

✓ I wrote different dialogue for each character.

✓ I expressed my ideas clearly.

Conventions

✓ I used quotations marks correctly.

Rob Hudson

A Class Trip

"I'm so glad our class visited the Children's Museum," said Maria. "What was your favorite part of the trip?"

"I liked seeing the children's toys. Some of them were more than a hundred and fifty years old," Henry answered.

"I liked that exhibit too. I didn't know kids played with dolls so long ago," said Maria. "The doll faces were hand-painted, too."

Henry smiled. "Can you imagine playing ball in those heavy shoes?" he asked.

Maria laughed. "No, I can't. But is was amazing to go back in time for a few hours."

107–108

Apply and Extend

Link the Readings

Copy the chart into your notebook. Read the words in the top row. Then follow these steps:

- For *Why Mosquitoes Buzz in People's Ears,* put an X under the words that remind you of the text.

- Repeat the same activity for *The Shoemakers and the Elves* and *John Henry and the Machine.*

	Informational text	Literature	Animal Characters	People Characters
Why Mosquitoes Buzz in People's Ears				
The Shoemakers and the Elves				
John Henry and the Machine				

Discussion

1. In *Why Mosquitoes Buzz in People's Ears* how do the characters **respond** to each other?

2. How do the shoemakers **react** when they discover the new shoes? What do they do?

3. How do the characters in the first two stories show that they care about each other?

 What do characters in tales have in common?

Listening Skills

If you can't hear someone, you can say, "Could you speak more loudly, please?"

Projects

Your teacher will help you choose one of these projects.

Written	Oral	Visual/Active
Character Sketch	**20 Questions**	**Book Cover**
Choose your favorite character from the selections. Describe the character. Tell why the character is your favorite.	With a partner, play 20 Questions. Choose a character from the unit. Your partner must ask you questions to try to identify the character.	Make a book cover for one of the selections. Include the title and the main character or characters on your cover.
Mixed-Up Tale	**Act It Out**	**Character Charades**
Choose one selection. Write a new version of the story. Include a character from one of the other selections.	Work with a group to perform *The Shoemakers and the Elves* for your classmates. Include props and costumes.	Play charades with a small group. Act out a character from the unit. Others must guess who your character is.

Further Reading

For more projects visit
LongmanCornerstone.com

 Hansel and Gretel
This Penguin Young Reader® is adapted from the classic Grimm's fairy tale. Tricked by their stepmother, Hansel and Gretel become lost in the forest. They discover a cottage in the woods. Will they ever find their way back home?

My Life with the Wave, Catherine Cowan
In this whimsical tall tale, a boy brings home an unusual friend—a wave from the sea. The boy and the wave share many adventures. But when the winter sets in, the wave becomes frozen and angry.

109–110

Perform a Play

You are going to write and perform a play. Then you will listen as your classmates perform a play, too.

❶ Prepare

A. Find two partners. Choose a short, well-known story or fairy tale. Then perform it as a play.

B. Discuss the story or fairy tale with your partners. Plan your play. Include a character for each of you. As you work together, listen to each other's ideas and work cooperatively. Now write your play. Discuss and find props and costumes to use in your play.

The Little Red Hen	
Little Red Hen:	Hello, Duck. Will you help me plant some seeds?
Duck:	No, Hen. I have to go swimming. Ask Dog.
Little Red Hen:	Hello, Dog. Will you help me plant some seeds?
Dog:	Sorry, Hen. I can't. I have to take my nap now. Ask Cat.
Little Red Hen:	Hi, Cat. Will you help me plant some seeds?
Cat:	Oh, no, Hen. Absolutely not. I just cleaned my fur. And planting seeds is such dirty work.

❷ Practice

Practice your play with your props. Perform it in front of your family or friends. If possible, record your play. Then listen to it. How do you and your partners sound? Record it again and try to improve.

❸ Present

As you speak, do the following:

- Have fun! Don't be nervous.
- Perform your play—don't read it.
- Pay attention to your partners, so you know when to say your lines.

As you listen, do the following:

- Watch the actions of the actors to help you understand.
- Pay close attention. Your teacher will ask you questions after the play.

❹ Evaluate

After you speak, answer these questions:

- ✔ Did you perform your play?
- ✔ Did you use props and costumes?

After you listen, answer these questions:

- ✔ Did you understand the play? Summarize it for a partner.
- ✔ Did you watch the actions of the actors?
- ✔ How did the actions help you understand the play?

Writing Workshop

Write a Story

Ongoing
Writing
Skills
Practice

Writing Prompt

Write a story that explains how or why something in the natural world came to be. Include characters, setting, conflict, and resolution.

❶ Prewrite

Review the writing you've done in this unit. Then choose a topic.
Think about how something in the natural world came to be.
What are the setting, characters, conflict, and resolution?
List your ideas in a graphic organizer.

A student named Ruth listed her ideas in this chart:

CHARACTERS Beaver, Dog	SETTING Time: Long Ago Place: Forest
CONFLICT (STRUGGLE) Beaver and dog want the same branch.	RESOLUTION (SOLUTION) Beaver gets stick so his teeth grow big and strong.

❷ Draft

Use your graphic organizer to write a draft.

- Keep your purpose in mind—to write a story.

- Include characters, setting, conflict, and resolution.

❸ Revise

Read over your draft. Look for places where the writing needs improvement. Use the Writing Checklist to help you. Then revise your draft.

Here is how Ruth revised her story:

Six Traits of Writing Checklist

✔ **Ideas**
Did I describe how something developed?

✔ **Organization**
Did the resolution follow the conflict?

✔ **Voice**
Does my tone suit my audience?

✔ **Word Choice**
Did I choose interesting details?

✔ **Sentence Fluency**
Did I vary my sentences?

✔ **Conventions**
Did I use quotation marks correctly?

Ruth Milan

How the Beaver Got Strong, Long Teeth

Long, long ago, a beaver had an idea.

"By building a dam across the stream, I can create a pond for my home. But I will need logs and branches," he thought.

He used his short, weak teeth to try to cut down a tree. After an hour of hard work, he managed to cut down one branch from the tree. "This is harder than I thought," he ~~thought.~~ said to himself.

Just then a dog sniffed at the branch. She tried to pull it away. "Find your own branch," the beaver shouted.

For two days the dog and the beaver tugged and tugged, until they fell asleep with the branch still in their mouths.

When the beaver woke up, the dog was gone. Picking up the branch, he realized ~~her~~ his teeth were very long and strong.

From that day on beavers have used their long, strong teeth to cut down trees.

Revised to correct error in mechanics.

Revised to use a variety of language.

Revised to correct spelling.

Revised to correct agreement of pronoun and possessive.

❹ Edit

Check your work for errors. Trade papers with a partner. Use the Peer Review Checklist to give each other feedback.

❺ Publish

Prepare a clean copy of your final draft. Share your essay with the class.

111–112

SPELLING TIP

Add -er to a word to mean *more* and -est to mean *most*.
low – lower – lowest
When a word ends in a silent *e*, you may need *to* add -r or -st.
wide – wider – widest

Listen to the sentences. Pay attention to the groups of words. Read aloud.

1. Mosquito's gossip causes mischief among the animals, so the lion never lets him talk again.

2. Two elves make shoes in secret to help an elderly couple.

3. Soon after the machine stopped, John Henry broke through the wall.

Work in pairs. Take turns reading aloud for one minute. Count the number of words you read.

One night, two elves are looking into the window of a	11
house where a shoemaker and his wife are inside. The elves	22
are tired and cold. They listen to the shoemakers talk	32
about their worries. The shoemakers have no leather for	41
shoes. They're afraid they'll have to close their shop.	50
The elves decide to sneak into the shop at midnight	60
and make lots of shoes in order to help the shoemakers.	71
Night after night, the elves continue to make shoes. The	81
shoemakers are speechless. They wonder who is helping them.	90
When they find out the truth, they leave clothes and food	101
for the elves. In the end, the shoemakers and the elves are	113
all happy.	115

With your partner, find the words that slowed you down.

- Practice saying each word and then say the sentence each word is in.
- Then take turns reading the text again. Count the number of words you read.

WB

113–114

Test Preparation

Taking Tests

You will often take tests that help show what you know. Follow these tips to improve your test-taking skills.

Coaching Corner

Answering Multiple-Choice Test Questions

- Many test items will give ask you to read a selection and then answer questions about it.

- The selections can be fiction or nonfiction. They can be long or short.

- Before you read the selection, preview the questions and answer choices.

- After reading the selection, first try to answer the question in your head.

- Look for the answer choice that matches the answer in your head.

- Check to make sure the answer you chose is supported by the text.

Read the following test sample. Study the tips in the box.

115–116

Read the selection. Then answer the questions.

1   Once upon a time, Dog and Cat lived together. Dog said, "We need to share the work. I'll go find food, if you will take care of the house." Cat agreed, and Dog went to find food.

2   Cat jumped up to the window, where the warm sunshine poured in. "I think I'll take a little nap before I work. "

3   Day after day, it was the same. Cat slept while Dog worked. Every day, Dog came home and said, "What did you do all day, Cat? The house is a mess!" Cat just yawned.

4   Then Dog got an idea. One day she told Cat she was going to work, but she hid under the sink instead. She watched Cat sleep all day. When Cat went to the sink to get a drink of water, Dog jumped out. "Yikes!" Cat screeched. Dog was furious and chased Cat around the room. That's how dogs started to chase cats.

1 What is Cat like?

   A Hungry

   B Lazy

   C Busy

   D Angry

2 Where did Dog hide?

   F Under the sink

   G At work

   H Behind the house

   J Under the bed

3 Why did Dog chase Cat?

   A Cat ate all the food.

   B Cat did not keep her promise.

   C Cat hurt Dog's feelings.

   D Cat screeched at Dog.

Tips

✔ Read the questions and answer choices before you read the selection.

✔ Eliminate choices that don't make sense.

Problem Solvers

You will read about how
people—and animals—
work to solve problems, from
out-of-control plants to
abandoned buildings.

Reading

1 | Photo Essay

**The Trouble
with Kudzu**

2 | Fables

**The Fox and the Crow
The Fox and the Goat**

3 | Social Studies

**New Life for Old
Buildings**

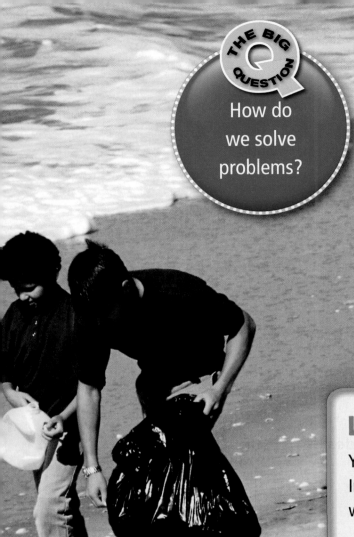

How do we solve problems?

Listening and Speaking

You will talk about problems and solutions. In the Listening and Speaking Workshop, you will give a speech.

Writing

You will practice persuasive writing. In the Writing Workshop, you will write a review.

Quick **Write**

What are some problems in your town? Write about one of them.

DVD   **VIEW AND RESPOND**
Talk about the poster for this unit. Then watch and listen to the video and answer the questions at <u>LongmanCornerstone.com</u>.

What do you know about problem solvers?

Words to Know

Listen and repeat. Use these words to talk about solving problems.

 brainstorm

 research

 debate

 investigate

 design

Work with a partner. Look up these words in a dictionary. Then ask and answer questions using these words and the words above.

doctor	student	lawyer	scientist

Example: A: How can a <u>scientist</u> solve problems?

B: A <u>scientist</u> can do <u>research</u> to solve problems.

Write

Read the question. Write your response in your notebook.

What are some things you do to solve problems?

Make Connections

Copy the sentences below into your notebook. Complete the sentences with the following words.

politicians

a detective

an architect

inventors

1. _____ often debate concerns or problems in their communities.

2. An _____ designs buildings. He or she often has to solve problems in creative ways.

3. _____ brainstorm new ideas together. They think of new things to invent and help each other solve problems that come up.

4. _____ has to investigate in order to solve crimes or mysteries.

What about you?

Talk about problems you have solved. How did you solve them?

Kids' Stories from around the World

the Netherlands

Sou Kor

Brian

I live in the Netherlands. Some of our parks have mazes made of hedges. There is only one correct path through the maze. I enter at one end and exit at the other. It's fun to get lost in a maze.

Suna

In South Korea people love to play Go. It is an old Chinese board game. You try to circle the other player's stones with your own. It's not easy, but it's fun!

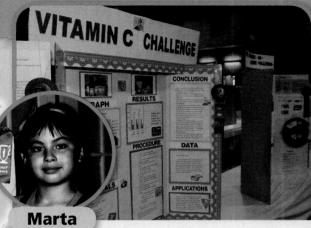

Canada

Texas, U.S.A.

Marta

My school is in Texas. Every year we have a science fair. I studied what happens if you don't get enough vitamins. Then I showed people my research. This year I won an award.

Arnoud

I live in Canada. My school has a new program. It teaches students to solve problems without fighting. I learn special skills, such as how to listen to others. I also learn to say what I feel without getting angry.

What about you?

1. What problems have you solved? How did solving them make you feel?

2. Do you know other stories about solving problems? Share your story with the class.

Reading 1

Prepare to Read

What You Will Learn

Reading

- Vocabulary building: *Context, phonics*

- Reading strategy: *Identify main idea and details*

- Text type: *Informational text (photo essay)*

Grammar
Comparatives

Writing
Write a persuasive business letter

These words will help you understand the reading.

Key Words

vine

bean

celebration

gardener

roots

Key Words

The Trouble with Kudzu tells about a plant from Japan that was given as a gift.

Words in Context

1 The **vine** is climbing up a wall. It is a plant with long stems.

2 A green **bean** is a type of seed that you can eat.

3 Parades are an important part of the **celebration** for the Chinese New Year.

4 In her backyard, the gardener plants vegetables and flowers.

5 The roots are underground and support the tree. They also help the tree get water.

Practice

Make flashcards to help you memorize the words.

- Write a key word on the front.
- On the back, make a drawing of each word.

Make Connections

What do you know about plants and trees? Have you ever planted a seed? Write your response in your notebook using some key words. Then discuss what you know with a partner.

Speaking Skills

When you don't know the right word to use, explain or describe the idea using words you know.

117

These words will help you talk about the reading.

Academic Words

affect
have an influence on

eliminate
remove or get rid of

outcome
final result

Academic Words

Words in Context Audio

The new classroom rules **affect** all the students.

Having a good plan at the beginning of a project will **eliminate** problems later.

Everyone wanted to know the **outcome** of Ari's science experiment.

Practice

Write the sentences in your notebook. Choose an academic word to complete each sentence.

1. I have to _____ peanut butter from my diet because I am allergic to peanuts.

2. One way to achieve the best _____ on a test is to study very hard.

3. You can _____ how people treat you by being kind and polite.

Apply

Ask and answer with a partner.

1. How does studying for a test **affect** your average at school?

2. What steps do you take to **eliminate** errors in what you write?

3. Explain the **outcome** of a project you finished at school. What was the final result?

118

Phonics

Soft and Hard c

Listen to your teacher read each word in the box. Then read each word aloud. Notice the difference between soft *c* and hard *c*.

Soft *c*	Hard *c*
celebrate	cake
decide	discuss
fancy	country

When does *c* have the same sound as the *s* in **sun**?
When does *c* have the same sound as the *k* in **kite**?

Rule

The letter *c* usually has the soft sound when it is followed by *e*, *i*, or *y*. Otherwise, *c* usually has the hard sound.

Practice

Use a word from the chart to match each clue.

1. It's what you do when you choose something. (soft *c*)
2. It's another word for nation. (hard *c*)
3. It's a sweet food you eat on your birthday. (hard *c*)
4. It's what you do for a special time. (soft *c*)
5. It's another word for talk. (hard *c*)

119

INFORMATIONAL TEXT

Photo Essay

More About

How can an unwanted plant cause problems?

 Listen to the Audio.
Listen for the main points and important details.

Reading Strategy

Identify Main Idea and Details

The main idea is the most important idea in the selection. The details give you information about the main idea. As you read ask yourself:

- What is the most important, or main, idea?
- What details help support the main idea?

Listen as your teacher models the reading strategy.

The Trouble with Kudzu

by Laura Sewel

Big, beautiful leaves and sweet-smelling purple flowers made kudzu popular.

This old truck is not going anywhere!

Do you know the story of Jack and the Beanstalk? Jack planted a magic bean . A vine grew from the bean. It grew and grew. Finally, the vine was so high and strong that Jack could climb up it and reach the clouds.

Well, kudzu doesn't come from a magic bean, but it is a member of the bean family. When people saw kudzu for the first time, they must have thought it was magic. Why? Because kudzu grows very fast—much faster than most other plants. In fact, it can grow up to 12 inches in only one day!

Before You Go On   After Jack planted the magic bean, what was the **outcome**?

Kudzu is a native plant of China and Japan. That means it grew naturally in those countries. Kudzu was brought to the United States from Japan in 1876 as a gift for a special celebration . The United States was celebrating its first 100 years as a **nation**.

Americans first saw kudzu at the 1876 **Centennial Exhibition** in Philadelphia.

Soon, every gardener and farmer wanted to plant kudzu seeds. Gardeners grew kudzu because it looked pretty and smelled good. Farmers grew it to feed their animals.

At first, kudzu was a big success! But it did not stop growing. It **blocked** sunlight that other plants needed. It killed trees and whole forests. Nothing was safe!

Centennial Exhibition   a show celebrating one hundred years

nation   country

blocked   stopped

Where have the trees gone? They are all covered with kudzu!

It takes only two or three years for kudzu to cover a house.

Now, people call kudzu a weed. It is a wild plant that grows where it is not wanted. People cut it down and dig up its roots. But **getting rid of** kudzu is not easy.

Over the years, people have learned to use every part of the kudzu plant. Cooks and artists use it to make jelly, paper, clothes, baskets, and chairs. This weed might be useful after all.

Artist Nancy Basket makes baskets with kudzu.

WB
120–122

getting rid of   removing completely

Reading Strategy

Identify Main Idea and Details

- What was the main idea?
- What were some details?
- How did thinking about the main idea help you understand the selection?

Think It Over

1. **Recall**   What are some ways that the kudzu plant is used today?

2. **Comprehend**   How did kudzu **affect** the forests? Explain.

3. **Analyze**   Why is it difficult to **eliminate** kudzu?

READING 1   **209**

Learning Strategies

Main Idea and Details

Identifying the **main idea and details** can help you understand what you read. Ask yourself, "What was the reading about?" Your answer is the main idea of the selection.

Read these sentences.

- Kudzu killed trees and whole forests.

- Kudzu is a wild plant that grows where it is not wanted.

- Gardeners grew kudzu because it looked pretty.

- Artists make baskets with kudzu.

- Kudzu blocked sunlight that other plants and trees needed.

1. Which sentence tells the main idea?

2. Which sentences tell the details that support the main idea?

Use a Main Idea and Details Chart

This chart can help you figure out the main idea of the selection. You can show the details that support the main idea.

 G.O. 141

Copy the chart. Fill in the main idea and details.

- Reread the selection. What is the main idea of *The Trouble with Kudzu*?

- Choose three of the most important details that support the main idea.

The main idea is:

_____

_____

Detail	Detail	Detail
_____	_____	_____
_____	_____	_____
_____	_____	_____

W B

123

Apply

Using the photographs, retell the selection to a partner.

Extension

Utilize Research and find out how to plant a seed. Write the steps. Explain them to a partner. Ask your partner to repeat the steps to show that he or she understands. Then switch roles and follow your partner's directions.

Grammar

Comparatives

When we compare or show the difference between two things, we use **comparative adjectives**.

Adjective	Comparative
It's a **fast** red car. ⟶	The red car is **fast**er than the blue car.
He made a **careful** step. ⟶	His step was more **careful** than hers.

To form the comparative, add *-er or more* to the adjective. But some adjectives have special spelling rules. Review these rules:

One-syllable adjectives
Add *-er*   **dark** ⟶ dark**er**
Ending in *-e*, add *-r*   wid**e** ⟶ wider
Ending in vowel + consonant, double the   fat ⟶ fat**ter**
   consonant and add *-er*

Two-syllable adjectives
Add *more*   **careful** ⟶ more careful
Ending in *-er, -le, -ow*, add *-(e)r*   gentl**e** ⟶ gentler
Ending in *-y*, change *-y* to *-i* and add *-er*   **happy** ⟶ happ**i**er

Three- or more syllable adjectives
Add *more* or *most*   **likable** ⟶ more likable

Irregular comparatives
good ⟶ better   far ⟶ farther
bad ⟶ worse   fun ⟶ more fun

In sentences, comparatives can be followed by *than*.

The cheetah is **fast**er **than** the lion.

**Change each adjective to a comparative. Write
the sentences.**

Example: The grape vines grew (high) _____
than ever before

The grape vines grew **higher** than
ever before.

1. It is (difficult) _____ to **eliminate** kudzu than other weeds.

2. Our new gardener is (skilled) _____ than the previous one.

3. This year's celebration will be (big) _____ than ever before.

4. We hope for a (good) _____ **outcome** this year.

5. I think the beans are (tasty) _____ than the peas.

Apply

**Work with a partner. Choose a topic from the box. Tell your partner
something you like (or dislike) related to each topic. Discuss your ideas.
Use comparative adjectives.**

Example: A: Cats are more interesting than dogs.

B: Oh, really? I think dogs are more fun.

W B

124

animals	sports	foods	games
colors	school subjects	seasons	famous people

**Grammar
Check ✓**

What are two
ways to form a
comparative?

Writing

Write a Persuasive Business Letter

In a persuasive business letter a writer tries to persuade someone to think or act in a certain way. Always include facts to support your ideas. Be sure to include all the parts of a business letter.

Writing Prompt

Write a persuasive business letter to someone in your community. Try to persuade that person to help solve a community problem. Be sure to use comparatives correctly.

❶ Prewrite

Choose someone to write to about a community problem.
Find the person's address. List your ideas in a graphic organizer.

A student named Tony listed his ideas like this:

> **Date**
> **Address of recipient**
> **Greeting**
> **Body**
> - Ask Ms. Hughes to donate art supplies.
> - Include facts to support my ideas.
> - End letter by thanking Ms. Hughes.
>
> **Closing**
> **Signature**

❷ Draft

Use your graphic organizer to help you write a first draft.
- Keep in mind your purpose for writing—to persuade.
- Include only the most important information.

❸ Revise

Read over your draft. Look for places where the writing needs improvement. Use the Writing Checklist to help you revise your draft.

❹ Edit

Check your work for errors. Use the Peer Review Checklist on page 402.

❺ Publish

Prepare a clean copy of your final draft. Share your paragraph with the class.

Here is Tony's business letter:

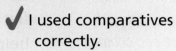

Writing Checklist

Ideas

✔ I included persuasive facts.

Organize

✔ I included all the parts of a business letter.

Conventions

✔ I used comparatives correctly.

WB

125–126

March 26, 2011

Ms. Kim Hughes

Hughes Arts Supply Store

41 First Avenue

New York, NY 10003

Dear Ms. Hughes:

The students at Webster School need art supplies. Without them, our art classes will be cancelled.

These classes are fun. Also, art skills are more important today than ever before. Research shows that workers with these skills can design more interesting ads, signs, commercials, and web sites. We should have more art classes, not fewer!

Your donation will enable our school to continue offering art classes.

Thank you for your time.

Sincerely,

Tony Liu

What You Will Learn

Reading

■ Vocabulary building: *Context, word study*

■ Reading strategy: *Compare and contrast*

■ Text type: *Literature (fables)*

Grammar
Superlatives

Writing
Write an advertisement

These words will help you understand the reading.

Key Words

flatter

praise

advice

guzzled

scampered

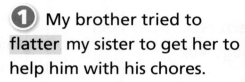

These fables are about a tricky fox.

Words in Context

1 My brother tried to **flatter** my sister to get her to help him with his chores.

2 My father gave me **praise** for the quality of my work. I received an A in math class.

3 Our **advice** to our little brother was this: do your homework every night.

4 After playing outside, the extremely thirsty dog eagerly guzzled all the water in his bowl.

5 The squirrel ran past us and quickly scampered up into the tree as we walked by.

Practice

Add a page to your vocabulary notebook.
- Divide your page into three columns: the new words, their definitions, and drawings of the words when possible.
- Test yourself by covering one of the columns.

Make Connections

Have you ever been tricked? What happened? How might you have stopped it from happening? Explain.

127

These words will help you talk about the reading.

WB
128

Academic Words

Academic Words

evaluate
judge how good something is

resourceful
good at finding ways to deal with problems effectively

scheme
tricky plan

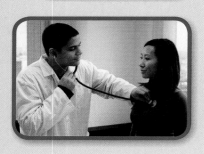

Words in Context

The doctor will **evaluate** your health during the examination.

We have to be creative and **resourceful** to get a good grade on our project.

The thief had a clever **scheme** to steal money from the company.

Practice

Write the sentences in your notebook. Choose an academic word to complete each sentence.

1. The pirates thought of a good _____ to steal the treasure.

2. If the teachers _____ your work and like what they see, you will get good grades.

3. Carlos showed how _____ he was by getting his mother, father, brother, and sister to help him with his homework.

Apply

Ask and answer with a partner.

1. How do your teachers **evaluate** your work at school?

2. Who do you know that's very **resourceful**?

3. Why does a villian's **scheme** make a story interesting?

Word Study

Thesaurus

A **dictionary** tells the meaning of a word. A **thesaurus** lists synonyms, or words with similar meanings, for a word.

Read this sentence.

> The fox escaped from the trap because he was very smart.

If you wanted to know the meaning of the word *smart*, you would look up the word in a dictionary. If you wanted to find a synonym for *smart*, a thesaurus would help you choose the best word. *Clever* is a synonym for the word *smart* and would be a good fit in this sentence.

Work with a partner.
- Read the sentence and the thesaurus entry that follows.
- Choose the synonym that could go in that sentence.

> "This is **bad** news," said the unlucky goat.

   bad *adj.* **1.** terrible. **2.** wrong. **3.** harmful. **4.** sick.

LITERATURE
Fables

More About

Why do some characters use tricks to solve their problems?

 Listen to the Audio.
Listen for the main points and important details.

Reading Strategy

Compare and Contrast

When you compare you see how things are similar. When you contrast you see how things are different. As you read the two stories think about how they are alike and different.

- Who are the characters in each story?
- How does Fox act in each story?
- What is the lesson each story teaches?

Listen as your teacher models the reading strategy.

The Fox and the Crow

an Aesop's fable retold by Lee Martin

One sunny, fall day, Mr. Fox went walking through the forest. "This would be a perfect afternoon," he said to himself, "except for my empty tummy." Echoing his thoughts, his stomach rumbled loudly.

Just then, Mr. Fox heard wings flapping overhead and he looked up to see a crow with a large piece of cheese in its beak. The crow landed in a tree nearby and Mr. Fox thought to himself, *That cheese looks very tasty. I must find a way to get it.* Being a clever fellow, he soon came up with an idea.

"Hello, Ms. Crow. Your feathers look especially **glossy** today and your eyes are as bright as glass beads."

---

glossy shiny

As Ms. Crow **cocked** her head, Mr. Fox knew he had her attention. He continued, "Your voice must be even more beautiful than the lovely picture you make sitting in that tree. I am sure if I could hear you sing, I would call you the Queen of All Birds!"

Pleased with Mr. Fox's praise, Ms. Crow took a deep breath and opened her beak to **caw.** Out fell the cheese, straight to the ground. Mr. Fox snapped it up.

"Yum! That is just what I needed, Ms. Crow. Let me offer you some advice : Do not trust someone whose words are meant only to flatter ."

---

cocked   tilted

caw   make a sharp, scratchy call, from a crow

Before You Go On   What was Mr. Fox's **scheme** for getting Ms. Crow to drop her cheese?

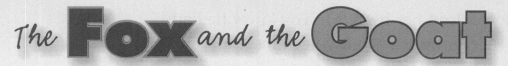

The Fox and the Goat

an Aesop's fable retold by Lee Martin

Mr. Fox fell into a **well** one day and could not find a way to get out. But just as he was about to give up hope, Mr. Goat looked over the edge of the well.

"Oh, I am so thirsty, Fox," he said. "Is the water good? And by the way, what are you doing in the well?"

Right away, Mr. Fox saw his chance to escape, so he said, "I am enjoying the water, of course! You should jump in and have a drink."

Without thinking, Mr. Goat jumped right into the well and guzzled the water noisily. After he had finished drinking, he looked at the smooth, steep walls of the well. "How will we get out of here?" he asked.

---

well   a deep hole that contains water and is often lined with stones

"Ahh," said Mr. Fox, "that is the problem, but I think I have an idea. If you put your front hooves on the wall, I will run up your back and out of the well. Then I will return to help you."

Mr. Goat did as Mr. Fox asked, and Mr. Fox scampered up his back and away as quickly as he could. He called back over his shoulder, "Goat, next time, you should look before you **leap**!"

---

leap jump

WB 130–132

Reading Strategy

Compare and Contrast

- Who are the characters in each story?

- How does Fox act in each story?

- **Evaluate** the lessons each story teaches. How are they similar? How are they different?

Think It Over

1. **Recall** Who did Mr. Fox fool in each story?

2. **Comprehend** How was Mr. Fox **resourceful** in solving his problems?

3. **Analyze** Why was Mr. Fox so successful in both stories?

Learning Strategies

Compare and Contrast

To understand what you read, compare and contrast ideas.

- When you **compare**, you tell how two or more things are alike.
- When you **contrast**, you tell how two or more things are different.

Practice

Compare and contrast the items listed in each exercise. Tell two ways they are alike. Then tell two ways they are different.

1. a fishbowl and a swimming pool

2. a car and a bicycle

3. a football and a basketball

Use a T-Chart

You can use a T-Chart to compare and contrast events, characters, or objects in a story or a non-fiction selection.

 **Practice**

Copy the T-Chart. Compare and contrast the stories.

1. Write about how *The Fox and the Crow* and *The Fox and the Goat* are the same. Use the pictures and the words in the selections.

2. Then write about how they are different.

3. Compare your completed T-Chart with a partner's.

How Are They Alike?	How Are They Different?

133

 **Apply**

Reread the story and take notes. Then close your book and retell the story to a partner. Use the key words as you speak.

Extension

Utilize Think about amusement park rides. Compare and contrast two rides. You can write descriptions, draw them, or act them out. Show your class how they are alike and how they are different.

Grammar

Superlatives

When we compare or show the difference between three or more things, we use **superlative adjectives**.

Adjective	Comparative	Superlative
rich	**rich**er	**rich**est
resourceful	more resourceful	most resourceful

To form the superlative, add -*est* or *most* to the adjective. This is similar to how we form comparatives.

One-syllable adjectives
Add *est*
Ending in -*e*, add -*st*
Ending in vowel + consonant,
   double the consonant and add -*est*

smart ——▶ smart**est**
nice ——▶ nic**est**
fit ——▶ fit**test**

Two-syllable adjectives
Add *most*
Ending in -*er*, -*le*, -*ow*, add -(*e*)*st*
Ending in -*y*, change -*y* to -*i*, add
  -*est*

pleasant ——▶ **most** pleasant
simple ——▶ simpl**est**
shiny ——▶ shin**iest**

Three or more syllable adjectives
Add *most*

exciting ——▶ **most** exciting

Irregular comparatives and superlatives

good ——▶ better ——▶ best

bad ——▶ worse ——▶ worst

A superlative is always preceded by the word *the*.

The cheetah is **the** **fastest** mammal of all.

Practice

Change each adjective to a superlative. Remember to add *the*. Write the sentences.

Example: The fox is (clever) <u>the cleverest</u> of
all of the animals.

1. Ms. Crow was  that her feathers were
   (glossy) _____.

2. The desert was (hot) _____ place on Earth.

3. The monkey easily scampered up (tall) _____ tree.

4. Her new **scheme** is (dangerous) _____ one yet.

5. Which scam was (tricky) _____?

Apply

Work with a partner. Read the sentences below and make statements. Use superlative adjectives.

Example: A: Rob is the shortest.

B: Juan is the tallest.

- Tim is shorter than Juan. Rob is shorter than Tim.

- Kara is funnier than Stella. But Stella is funnier than Maria.

- Your house is bigger than mine. But his house is bigger
  than yours.

134

- Kevin is wise. Max is wiser than Kevin.
  Marta is wiser than both of them.

- The forest is much more peaceful than
  the beach. The mountains aren't quite as
  peaceful as the forest.

Grammar Check ✓

When do we use
superlative adjectives?

Writing

Write an Advertisement

Advertisements persuade people to buy products. Short
sentences include important details and facts that will appeal to
buyers. These details describe the most important features of
the product.

Writing Prompt

Write an advertisement about a real or imaginary product you
can use in your home or school. Include important details and facts to
persuade people to buy the products. Be sure to use
superlatives correctly.

❶ Prewrite G.O. 153

Choose a product to
write about. Think
about the words you
will use to describe the
most important features
of this product. List your
ideas in a word web.

A student named Ana listed her ideas in
this word web:

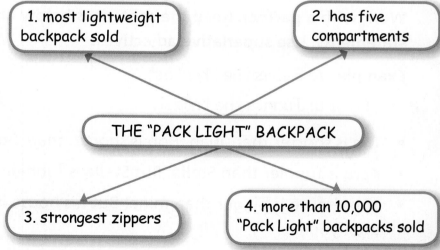

1. most lightweight backpack sold

2. has five compartments

THE "PACK LIGHT" BACKPACK

3. strongest zippers

4. more than 10,000 "Pack Light" backpacks sold

❷ Draft

Use your word web to
help you write a first draft.

- Keep in mind your purpose for writing—to create an
  interesting ad.
- Include details that describe the features of the product.

❸ Revise

Read over your draft. Look for places where the sentences are too long or the details are not interesting. Use the Writing Checklist to help you identify problems. Then revise your draft.

❹ Edit

Check your work for errors. Trade papers with a partner to get feedback. Use the Peer Review Checklist on page 402. Edit your final draft in response to feedback from your partner and your teacher.

❺ Publish

Prepare a clean copy of your final draft. Share your paragraph with the class. Save your work.

Here is Ana's ad for a backpack:

Writing Checklist

Ideas

✔ I included interesting details to appeal to buyers.

✔ I wrote short sentences to clearly explain my ideas.

Conventions

✔ I used superlatives correctly.

Ana Yang

The "Pack Light" is today's newest backpack!
- It's the most lightweight backpack sold!
- It has five different compartments!
- It's easy to pack and unpack!
- Its zippers are the strongest!
- More than 10,000 "Pack Lights" sold!

Carrying a "Pack Light" makes a difference. Be the coolest kid in class. Buy one today.

135–136

What You Will Learn

Reading

- Vocabulary building: *Context, phonics*
- Reading strategy: *Identify cause and effect*
- Text type: *Informational text (social studies)*

Grammar

Adverbs of frequency and intensity

Writing

Write a persuasive brochure

These words will help you understand the reading.

Key Words

communities

preserve

architects

original

concerned

purpose

Key Words

New Life for Old Buildings is about saving and fixing old buildings.

Words in Context

1 Many communities have lots of businesses and services, such as shopping centers and restaurants.

2 The mayor wanted to preserve the old building, but others didn't want to save it.

3 Skilled architects designed and drew up construction plans for our new house.

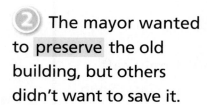

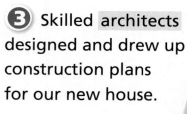

4 The original flag of the United States had just 13 stars. Now our flag has 50 stars.

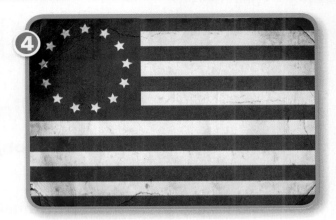

5 My mother was concerned for my brother when he was sick and had a fever.

6 The purpose of the food drive was to fill the food pantry shelves and help feed hungry people.

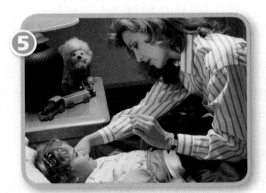

Make flashcards for the words.

- Write a key word on the front.

- On the back, write a sentence, but leave a blank where the key word should be.

- Use the cards to quiz yourself.

Make Connections

Can you think of an old building that you like? Why do you like it? How do people use this building? Write your answers in your notebook.

WB

137

These words will help you talk about the reading.

Academic Words

objective
goal

restore
repair something to make it seem new again

site
place

Academic Words

Words in Context Audio

The cook's **objective** was to create a healthy and tasty meal.

The watchmakers fix and **restore** old, broken watches.

The fire trucks rushed to the **site** of the fire.

Practice

Write the sentences in your notebook. Choose an academic word to complete each sentence.

1. Sue's _____ was to win the race.

2. The _____ of the battle no longer showed any signs that people had fought there.

3. We couldn't _____ the old boat; it had too many holes in it.

Apply

Ask and answer with a partner.

1. Why is it a good idea to write your **objective** before starting a task?

2. Do you own something old that you want to **restore**?

3. What might be a good **site** for a vegetable garden at your school?

Phonics

Digraph: *ow*

Sometimes the letters *ow* make one sound. Listen. Sound out the words in the box.

Words with digraph *ow*	
grow	cow
own	down
yellow	tower

What two vowel sounds do the letters *ow* have? Say the words in the box aloud.

Rule

The letters *ow* can have the long *o* sound you hear in **grow** or the vowel sound you hear in **how**. Some words, such as **bow**, have two meanings and can be pronounced either way.

Practice

Read the sentences with a partner. Look for words with *ow*.

- Not long ago, people tore down old buildings.
- They can show visitors what life was like in the past.
- Now communities are trying to preserve old buildings.

1. List the words in which **ow** has the long **o** sound heard in **show**.

2. List the words in which **ow** has the short **o** sound heard in **cow**.

139

More About

What problems do we solve by using old things in new ways?

Audio **Listen to the Audio.**
Listen for the main points and important details.

Reading Strategy

Identify Cause and Effect

What makes an event happen is a cause. The result of a cause is an effect.

- Identify what caused some buildings to be saved.
- Identify some effects of saving the old buildings.

Listen as your teacher models the reading strategy.

New life for OLD BUILDINGS

by Maria Coulter

You might be surprised to know that buildings are like people in some ways. Like people, they have a story to tell. Like each person, each building has a past.

Now, communities are trying to preserve their old buildings. Factories, train stations, churches, and schools are getting new lives!

Have you ever visited an old building and wondered about its history? Did you try to picture who lived or worked there? Imagine visiting an art gallery that was once a **jail**. Now it holds art instead of prisoners.

---

jail   place where criminals are kept when they are punished

One hundred years ago, Union Station in St. Louis was the largest and busiest railroad station in the world. Today, it is a hotel with shops, restaurants, and offices.

Andrew Carnegie gave money to the City of Franklin to build this new library.

Not long ago, people tore down old buildings that were no longer **suitable** for their original purposes. Usually, they **replaced** old buildings with new ones. Sometimes they just left empty lots. When these buildings came down, people lost important **links** to the past.

---

suitable right or acceptable

replaced put something new in the place of something broken or old

links things that connect something with something else

Before You Go On How might people use an old building site in new ways?

People in Littleton, Colorado, built this train station in 1888. It was empty for years. Then it became the Depot Art Center and Gallery.

In Delray, Florida, people turned an elementary school into the Cornell Museum of Art and History.

People have learned that they can use an old building for a new purpose. Concerned **citizens** are finding creative ways to reuse buildings. **Mansions** have become museums. Schools have become apartment buildings. Railroad stations have become shopping centers.

---

citizens   people who live in a certain place

mansions   large houses owned by rich people

Museums preserve objects from the past. This weaver's loom was used to make cloth.

There are good reasons to salvage old buildings.

Many old buildings were made with stone and brick. They are often strong and beautiful. Architects designed them to last a long time.

Vacant buildings are a problem in urban and rural areas. **Rescuing** these buildings is a popular **solution**.

---

rescuing saving

solution way to solve a problem

This strong building is being restored.

140–142

Reading Strategy

Identify Cause and Effect

As you read this selection, you looked for causes and effects.

- What examples of causes and effects did you identify?

- Did looking for causes and effects help you to understand the selection?

Think It Over

1. **Recall** What is one type of building that is often used in a new way?

2. **Comprehend** What is the main **objective** for people who want to protect old buildings?

3. **Analyze** How does giving an old building a new use help **restore** and save that building?

Learning Strategies

Cause and Effect

Finding cause and effect relationships can help you to understand what you read.

- The **cause** is what makes something happen.
- The **effect** is the result of the cause.

To find an effect in a story, ask yourself: "What happened?"
To find the cause, ask yourself: "Why did this happen?"

Practice

Read the sentences below with a partner.

- Make a chart with two columns. Write "Cause" in one column. Write "Effect" in the other column.
- List each cause and each effect in the correct column.

1. The water started to boil. Katie heated the tea kettle.

2. Stan studies every day. Stan does well on quizzes.

3. The baseball broke the window. Tom hit the baseball.

4. Plants grew in the field. The farmer planted the seeds.

Use a Cause and Effect Chart

You can use a cause and effect chart to help you
understand cause and effect relationships in a story.

 G.O. 148

**Copy and complete this Cause and Effect Chart
for *New Life for Old Buildings*. Then compare
your completed chart with a partner's.**

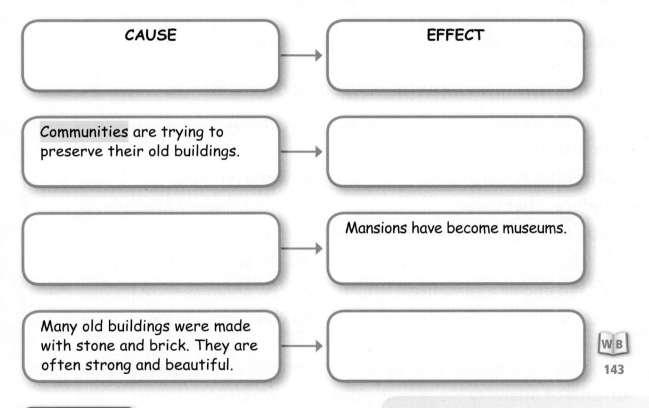

CAUSE	EFFECT
Communities are trying to preserve their old buildings. →	
→	Mansions have become museums.
Many old buildings were made with stone and brick. They are often strong and beautiful. →	

WB
143

Apply

**Take notes on the selection. Share them
with a partner.**

Extension

Utilize Are people using
old buildings in your
neighborhood in new ways? Are
there any buildings you would
like to see **restored** and saved?
Tell your class about them.

Grammar

Adverbs of Frequency and Intensity

Adverbs tell *when, where, why,* or *how* something is done. Many adverbs end in *-ly*, like *usually*, but others do not, such as *never*.

Adverbs of frequency describe time. They answer the question *How often?* They range from *always* to *never*:

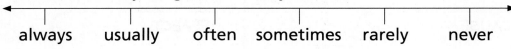

| always | usually | often | sometimes | rarely | never |

Notice the position of adverbs of frequency in a sentence:

Position	
After the *be* verb	She **is** never late.
Before other verbs	We always **study** after school.
For *usually* and *sometimes*	
At the beginning of a sentence	Usually we go to the beach.
At the end of a sentence	We see dolphins sometimes.
Before the main verb in a question	**Do you** always bring your lunch?

Adverbs of intensity describe the degree to which something was done. They answer the question, *How much?*

Adverbs	**Position**	
very, too, really	Before the adjective or adverb	I ran very **fast** this time.

Fill in the blanks with an adverb of frequency or intensity. Use the words in the box.

always	rarely
never	very
usually	often

Example: Old buildings are <u>often</u> used for a new purpose .

1. They are _____ happy that they achieved their **objective**.

2. Sometimes our after school group is so large that we can _____ meet in one classroom.

3. Our community works very hard so we are _____ successful.

4. We _____ try our very best!

5. They _____ **restored** that old building, so it was torn down.

Work with a partner. Make statements about your schedule and things you do. Use the following words in your statements.

always	rarely	very
usually	never	too
sometimes	often	really

144

Example: A: I always eat breakfast at home.
Sometimes I bring my lunch to school.
B: I never eat breakfast. I usually bring my lunch. Sometimes I buy it.

Grammar Check ✓

What do adverbs of frequency tell us? What do adverbs of intensity tell us?

Writing

Write a Persuasive Brochure

A brochure is a small book about a topic. A persuasive brochure convinces someone to act or think in a certain way. Clear details present information that will persuade the reader.

Writing Prompt

Write a persuasive brochure to encourage people to attend an event in your community. Include all the necessary information about the event. Use clear, interesting details to present the information in a persuasive way. Be sure to use adverbs of frequency and intensity correctly.

❶ Prewrite

Choose an event to write about. Think about the information that will persuade readers to attend. List the information in a graphic organizer.

A student named Sam listed his ideas like this:

> **PAGE 1**
> • Separate dog runs for large and small dogs.
> • Dog run to be cleaned frequently.
> • Dogs must be well behaved.

> **PAGE 2**
> • Date + time: Friday, September 10 at 9 A.M.
> • Place: Morris Park Dog Run, 205 Morris Avenue

❷ Draft

Use your story board to help you write a first draft.

- Keep in mind your purpose for writing—to persuade.
- Show interesting details to appeal to your readers.

❸ Revise

Read over your draft. Look for places where the writing needs improvement. Use the Writing Checklist to help you identify problems. Then revise your draft.

❹ Edit

Check your work for errors. Trade papers with a partner to get feedback. Use the Peer Review Checklist on page 402.

❺ Publish

Prepare a clean copy of your final draft. Share your paragraph with the class. Save your work.

Writing Checklist

Ideas

✓ I included information about the event.

✓ I used interesting details to persuade the reader.

Conventions

✓ I used adverbs of frequency and intensity correctly.

Here is Sam's brochure:

Sam Yi

[page 1] Come to the opening of the Morris Park dog run.

It has separate dog runs for large and small dogs.

• The dog run will be cleaned frequently.

• All dogs must be well behaved.

• If dogs bark too loudly, they will have to leave.

[page 2] Please mark the opening on your calendar!

• Friday, September 10 at 9 A.M.

• Morris Park Dog Run, 205 Morris Avenue

We will be very pleased to welcome you and your dog!

145–146

Apply and Extend

Link the Readings

Copy the chart into your notebook. Read the words in the top row. Then follow these steps:

- For *The Trouble with Kudzu*, put an X under the words that remind you of the text.

- Repeat the same activity for *The Fox and the Crow* and *The Fox and the Goat* and *New Life for Old Buildings*.

	Informational text	Literature	Solution helps one character	Solution helps many
The Trouble with Kudzu				
The Fox and the Crow and The Fox and the Goat				
New Life for Old Buildings				

Discussion

1. The title of the story is *The Trouble with Kudzu*. Does kudzu still cause trouble? Why or why not?

2. How did Mr. Fox's actions **affect** the other characters in the stories? How did Andrew Carnegie **affect** people's lives?

3. How does **restoring** old buildings solve problems?

 How do we solve problems?

Projects

Your teacher will help you choose one of these projects.

Written	Oral	Visual/Active
Skit	**Fable**	**Flowchart of Steps**
Choose one of the selections. Write a skit about the problem and how it was solved. Make sure the problem and solution are clear.	Many fables are about solving a problem. The way a character solves a problem leads to a lesson. Write a fable about someone who must solve a problem.	Think of a problem you read about and how it was solved. Identify the problem. Tell what steps were taken to solve it. Then explain the solution.
News Article	**Interview**	**Comic Strip**
Write a newspaper article about a problem that you heard about. Tell how people solved it. Answer the 5 W questions in your article.	Interview someone who has solved a problem. Find out what the problem was. Tell how the person solved it. Record your interview.	Create a comic strip about a problem and how it is solved. Use a problem you read about, or think of your own problem.

For more projects visit
LongmanCornerstone.com

Further Reading

Peter and the Wolf, retold by Lynne Doherty Herndon
This Penguin Young Reader® is a classic. Peter, with the help of a bird and a cat, uses clear thinking and courage to capture a scary wolf.

The Brand New Kid, Katie Couric
In this rhyming story, the new kid in school is having trouble fitting in. That is, until someone befriends him and tells others what an interesting kid he is.

147–148

Give a Speech

You are going to write and give a speech. Then you will listen as your classmates give a speech.

❶ Prepare

A. Choose a problem that has been solved. It can be from your school, your community, or somewhere else in the world. Research it and give a speech based on your research.

B. Think about what you want to tell your classmates. You will need to describe the problem, tell about the person who solved it, and explain how the person solved the problem. Find photos, posters, or other props to show during your speech.

> **The Center for Community**
>
> The small, old jail on Freedom Road was a big, new problem. It was empty and falling down. It was a dangerous place, too, with broken glass and rusty nails everywhere. Parents in our community worried about their children because they were playing there. Something had to be done. Tonya Jones, the new major, promised to fix the problem. This is what

❷ Practice

Practice your speech with your props. Practice in front of your family or friends. If possible, record your speech. Then listen to yourself. How do you sound? Record yourself again and try to improve.

❸ Present

As you speak, do the following:
- Face your audience and relax.
- Speak clearly and take your time.
- Show your props and other visuals.

As you listen, do the following:
- Listen for the general meaning, main point, and any details.
- Pay close attention. Your teacher will ask you questions about the speech.

❹ Evaluate

After you speak, answer these questions:
- ✔ Did you describe the problem clearly?
- ✔ Did you explain who solved it and how?

After you listen, answer these questions:
- ✔ Did you know anything about the problem before the speech?
- ✔ Did the speaker use formal or informal language?
- ✔ Think about the general meaning of the speech. Can you think of a title for it? Tell your idea to the class.

Writing Workshop

Write a Review

Writing Prompt

Write a review of a book, movie, or play. Clearly express your opinion of the work and include reasons that support your view.

❶ Prewrite

Review your writing for this unit. Then think of a movie, play, or book that you liked or disliked. Why did you feel as you did? List your ideas in a graphic organizer.

A student named Rob listed his ideas in this chart:

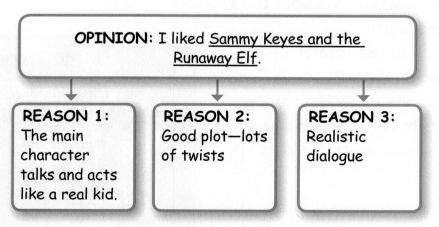

OPINION: I liked <u>Sammy Keyes and the Runaway Elf</u>.

REASON 1: The main character talks and acts like a real kid.

REASON 2: Good plot—lots of twists

REASON 3: Realistic dialogue

❷ Draft

Use your graphic organizer to write a draft.

• Keep your purpose in mind—to write a review.

• Support your opinion with reasons.

❸ Revise

Read over your draft. Look for places where the writing needs improvement. Use the Writing Checklist to help you. Then revise your draft.

Here is how Rob revised his review.

Six Traits of Writing Checklist

✔ **Ideas**
Did I clearly express my opinion?

✔ **Organization**
Did I give reasons for my opinion?

✔ **Voice**
Does my writing sound like me?

✔ **Word Choice**
Did I choose specific words?

✔ **Sentence Fluency**
Did I use different kinds of sentences?

✔ **Conventions**
Did I begin and end sentences correctly?

Rob Park

I enjoyed reading <u>Sammy Keyes and the Runaway Elf</u> by Wendelin Van Draanen. This mystery begins, when 13-year-old Sammy agrees to take care of a dog during the Christmas parade in her hometown. The tiny dog, named Marique, jumps off a parade float and is kidnapped. The dog's owner hires Sammy to find the kidnappers. Sammy looks everywhere — ~~including~~ even in a garbage can. By the end of the book, Sammy cracks the case and finds the dog. She also learns why a young girl, the runaway elf, is so unhappy.

Sammy talks and acts like a real kid does. The plot was exciting, with enough twists to keep me ~~involved~~ guessing. The dialogue is sharp. As you read, you feel that Sammy, the narrator, is talking directly to you.

Sammy's a funny, smart person I liked knowing. I think you will, too.

Revised to correct mechanics.

Revised to clarify meaning.

Revised to make writing smoother.

Revised to make more vivid.

❹ Edit

Check your work for errors. Trade papers with a partner. Use the Peer Review Checklist to give each other feedback.

❺ Publish

Prepare a clean copy of your final draft. Share your essay with the class.

149–150

SPELLING TIP

The /k/ sound can be spelled with the letter *c*, *k*, or *ck*.

book cave track

Use a dictionary to check the spelling of words with the /k/ sound.

Listen to the sentences. Pay attention to the groups of words. Read aloud. Audio

1. Kudzu doesn't come from a magic bean, but it is a member of the bean family.

2. One sunny, fall day, Mr. Fox went walking through the forest.

3. Now communities are trying to preserve old buildings and use them for new purposes.

Work in pairs. Take turns reading the passage below aloud for one minute. Count the number of words you read.

Kudzu is a native plant of China and Japan. That	10
means it grew naturally in those countries. Kudzu was	19
brought to the United States from Japan in 1876 as a	30
gift for a special celebration. The United States was	39
celebrating its first 100 years as a nation.	47
Soon, every gardener and farmer wanted to plant kudzu	56
seeds. Gardeners grew kudzu because it looked pretty and	65
smelled good. Farmers grew it to feed their animals.	74
At first, kudzu was a big success! But it did not stop	86
growing. It blocked sunlight that other plants needed. It	95
killed trees and whole forests. Nothing was safe!	103
Now, people call kudzu a weed. It is a wild plant	114
that grows where it is not wanted.	121

With your partner, find the words that slowed you down.

- Practice saying each word and then say the sentence each word is in.
- Then take turns reading the text again. Count the number of words you read.

151–152

Test Preparation

Taking Tests

You will often take tests that help show what you know. Follow these tips to improve your test-taking skills.

Coaching Corner

Answering Test Items for Revising and Editing

- Revising and Editing Tests often ask you to look for corrections and improvements that a writer should make.

- Before you read the written selection, preview the questions and answer choices.

- Read the whole selection carefully.

- After reading the selection, go back and carefully reread the sentences mentioned in the questions. Do you notice any mistakes in grammar or punctuation?

- Read each of the answer choices to yourself to see if one of them sounds better than the sentence in the selection. Choose the answer that does the most to improve the whole sentence.

- Remember that sometimes the sentence will not need any corrections.

Read the following test sample. Study the tips in the box.

153–154

Ruby wrote this paragraph about skateboarding. Read her work and look for any corrections and improvements she should make. Answer the questions that follow.

(1) At tonight's town meeting, the City Council will announce its decision to make skateboarding on the sidewalk against the law. (2) Too many skateboarders have run into people and cars. (3) These accidents are making people verry angry. (4) But responsible skateboarders are angry, too. (5) Parents of skateboarders may be angryier than the kids. (6) They will have to pay fines if their kids are caught skateboarding on the sidewalk. (7) Mr. Ikeda has offered to give the town a plot of land to build a skateboard park. (8) It's a great offer, but we need money to build it. (9) Come to the town meeting, and share your ideas!

1 What change, if any, should be made in sentence 3?

    A Change *accidents* to **accident**

    B Change *are* to **is**

    C Change *These* to **This**

    D Change *verry* to **very**

2 Which change, if any, is needed in sentence 5?

    F Change *Parents* to **Parents'**

    G Change *are* to **is**

    H Change *angryier* to **angrier**

    J Make no change

3 What change, if any, should be made in sentence 9?

    A Change *share* to **say**

    B Change *Come* to **Came**

    C Delete **meeting**

    D Make no change

Tips

✔ Think about what you have learned about adverbs of intensity.

✔ Review what you know about forming comparatives.

Where We Live

You will learn about different
types of homes and the people
who live in them.

Reading

1 | Article

**The Underground
City**

2 | Letters

A House of Grass

3 | Biography

**A Young Pioneer
in Kansas**

THE BIG QUESTION

What is it like to live in an unusual home?

Listening and Speaking

You will talk about places to live. In the Listening and Speaking Workshop, you will present a TV talk show.

Writing

You will practice expository writing. In the Writing Workshop, you will write a magazine or newspaper article.

Quick Write

Where do you live? What is your home like? Describe it.

DVD

VIEW AND RESPOND
Talk about the poster for this unit. Then watch and listen to the video and answer the questions at LongmanCornerstone.com.

What do you know about places to live?

Words to Know

Listen and repeat. Use these words to talk about places to live.

townhouse

apartment

mobile home

houseboat

retirement home

single-family home

Practice

Work with a partner. Ask questions using the words above.
Answer them using words from the box or your own ideas.

cousin	friend	uncle	aunt	grandparents

Example: A: Do you know anyone that lives in a <u>retirement home</u>?

B: Yes, my <u>grandparents</u> live in a <u>retirement home</u>.

Write

Read the questions. Write your response in your notebook.

Where do you live? Who do you live with?

Make Connections

Copy the sentences below into your notebook. Complete the sentences with the following phrases.

play on the swings

swim in the water

ride an elevator

eat dinner

1. My uncle lives on a houseboat. We like to ____ when we visit him.

2. My grandparents live in a retirement home. They ____ in a dining hall with many friends.

3. My friend Ava lives in a single-family home. In the backyard we like to ____ .

4. My parents and I live in an apartment. We live on the fifth floor, so every day we ____ .

What about you?

Talk with a partner. Talk about your home.

Kids' Stories from around the World

China

New Guinea

Xiaohong

I live in China. Many families here live on boats. My family has a houseboat. We have a fishing business. My father and my brother take the boat into the ocean. They catch fish. Then they return to the harbor. I eat the fish they bring home.

Rabbie

I live in Papua New Guinea. In my country, some people live in treehouses. Some families live in trees that are 80 feet high! I live in a house on the ground. But I hope to live in a treehouse one day.

Scotland

Iowa, U.S.A.

Jemma

I live in Scotland, near a very interesting house. It's called "the Pineapple." It was built in 1761. Its stone top looks like a giant pineapple. Today, people rent the house for vacations. I want to stay there. Then I can say I slept in a pineapple.

Carlito

I live in Iowa. People come from far away to see the "spaceship house" in my town. The house has a round room that is 57 feet long. It looks just like a spaceship. I think it would be fun to live in this house!

What about you?

1. Which house would you like to live in? Explain why.

2. Do you have a story about an unusual home? Share your story.

Prepare to Read

What You Will Learn

Reading

- Vocabulary building: *Context, word study*

- Reading strategy: *Identify fact and opinion*

- Text type: *Informational text (magazine article)*

Grammar

Capitalizing proper nouns

Writing

Write to classify

These words will help you understand the reading.

Key Words

native

extreme

architecture

underground

mining

efficient

Key Words

The Underground City tells about a town where people live in caves.

Words in Context

① Kangaroos are native to Australia. They live in the wild there. Kangaroos are not native to the United States. You can only find them in zoos.

② The United States is a big country. Some parts have extreme, or great, heat. Other parts have extreme cold.

3 Styles of architecture change with time. Look at these two museums. Which one is an older style? How do you know?

4 Coal and gold are found underground. They are deep under Earth's surface. We get them by mining. Workers dig down to where the coal or gold is. Then they bring it up to the surface.

5 Being efficient means working quickly and well. When you are efficient, you do not waste time.

Practice

Add a page to your vocabulary notebook.

- Divide your page into three columns: the new words, their definitions, and drawings of the words when possible.
- Test yourself by covering one of the columns.

Speaking Skills

If you don't know the exact English word, use a synonym.

Make Connections

Have you ever been in a cave? Describe how it feels. Was it warm or cold? Was it damp or dry? Why do you think some people like living in caves?

155

These words will help you talk about the reading.

Academic Words

adapt
change to fit a new situation

environment
world of land, sea, and air that you live in; your surroundings

located
be in a particular place

Academic Words

Words in Context

Wolves **adapt** to cold weather by growing a thick coat.

Recycling paper and plastic is good for the **environment**.

The park is **located** near the school.

Practice

Write the sentences in your notebook. Choose an adademic word to complete each sentence.

1. Buffalo is _____ in the state of New York.

2. After we move to a new town it took some time to _____ to it.

3. Trees, water, and air are all part of our _____ .

Apply

Ask and answer with a partner.

1. Think of a time when you visited a new place. How did you **adapt** to it?

2. Where was the new place **located**?

3. How was the **environment** different there than at home?

Word Study

Homophones

How are the words in red alike?
How are they different?

> Do the stores **sell** opals?
> Is there a jail **cell** in town?

The words *sell* and *cell* sound the same, but they have different spellings and different meanings. They are **homophones**.
- In the first sentence, *sell* means "to exchange for money."
- In the second sentence, *cell* means "a small room in a jail."

Practice

Write each sentence. Use the correct homophone.

1. I _____ like to visit Australia. (wood, would)

2. I want to meet the people who live _____. (their, there)

3. We will _____ the miners at work. (sea, see)

4. She might _____ an opal. (buy, by)

5. I can hardly _____ him. (hear, here)

6. _____ coming to the party aren't you? (your, you're)

INFORMATIONAL TEXT
Magazine Article

More About

Why is it important that people and animals **adapt** their homes to their **environment**?

 Listen to the Audio.
Listen for the main points and important details.

Reading Strategy

Identify Fact and Opinion

- A fact is something that is true. You can prove something is a fact.

- An opinion is something that someone thinks is true but cannot be proven.

- As you read, think about what is a fact and what is an opinion.

Listen as your teacher models the reading strategy.

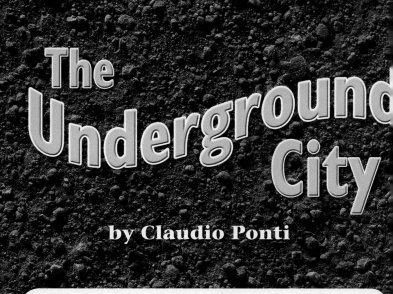

The Underground City

by Claudio Ponti

Have you ever seen a house that is under the ground? Come visit a town called Coober Pedy!

The town of Coober Pedy is in southern Australia.

A man plays a game in his underground home.

About 3,500 people live in Coober Pedy, Australia. From the street, you might see only dirt and some trees. But under the ground, there are homes! More than half of the people in the town live in underground houses. These are regular houses that look a lot like yours!

The summer heat in Coober Pedy is extreme. But the underground homes are efficient. They stay cool during the hot months. That means people don't spend money on air conditioning. In the winter, the homes stay warm. That means people pay less for heat.

The underground houses look just like regular homes.

Before You Go On How did the people of Coober Pedy **adapt** to the extreme heat?

Opals are beautiful gems that are used for jewelry.

Reading **Skill**

Ask your teacher or classmates if you don't understand a word, phrase, or a language structure.

Opals are native to Coober Pedy. Most of the people who live there work in the opal **business**. They dig up opals from under the ground. Then they sell the opals to people all over the world.

The first opal was found in Coober Pedy in 1915. Soon, mining became popular there. The miners noticed how cool the air was inside the mines. These men had slept in **trenches** in World War I, so they knew that living under the ground was cooler than living in the **desert** heat. That's how the underground homes began.

business   buying or selling of goods and services

trenches   long, narrow holes dug into the ground

desert   large area of land that is very dry and usually very hot

Soldiers in World War I lived in trenches below the ground.

In Coober Pedy, people dig out dirt and leave it in big piles.

From: Meghan@example.com
To: Max@example.com
Subject: Coober Pedy

Hello Max,

I am in Coober Pedy. It is a special town in Australia. Many **visitors** come to see the underground architecture. The people who live in Coober Pedy work hard in the heat all day. They spend many hours drilling for opals. At the end of the day, they go to their nice, cool homes. They live in underground caves!

I'll see you soon!

Meghan

I saw workers use large machines to dig opals out of the ground.

158–160

---

visitors people who come to see a place or a person

Reading Strategy

Identify Fact and Opinion

- What is one fact about Coober Pedy?
- What is one opinion of Coober Pedy?
- Did looking for facts and opinions help you understand the selection? How?

Think It Over

1. **Recall** Where is Coober Pedy **located**?

2. **Comprehend** How do the people who live in Coober Pedy **adapt** to the heat?

3. **Analyze** How is the **environment** of Coober Pedy different from the environment where you live?

Learning Strategies

Fact and Opinion

A **fact** is something that can be proved. An **opinion** is something that someone thinks, but which cannot be proven. Words such as *great, amazing,* and *bad* are clues that you are reading opinions.

Practice

Tell whether each sentence states a fact or an opinion. If it is a fact, tell where you can find the proof.

1. The town of Coober Pedy is **located** in Australia.
2. It is hard to live underground.
3. About 3,500 people live in Coober Pedy.
4. People who live underground are friendly.
5. The temperature of underground homes is under 72 degrees Fahrenheit in the summer.

Use a Fact and Opinion Chart

A Fact and Opinion Chart can help you tell facts from opinions.

Sort the list of facts and opinions from the previous page.
Explain your choice in the third column. Then answer the
questions below.

Fact	Opinion	Why?
The town of Coober Pedy is located in Australia.		You can prove it by looking on a map of Australia.
	It is hard to live underground.	The word **hard** is a clue that this is an opinion.

1. Which sentence would you add to the Fact column?
   a. Opals are beautiful gems.
   b. The first opal was found in Coober Pedy in 1915.
   c. People who live underground are friendly.
   d. Coober Pedy is a special town.

2. How could you prove the fact
   that you chose?
   a. Ask a friend.
   b. Look it up in an encyclopedia.
   c. Read about it in a newspaper.
   d. Buy an opal.

161

Summarize the selection for a partner.
Use the key words as you speak.

Extension

Utilize Would you like to live
underground? Make a drawing
that shows what your house
would look like. Share your
drawing with the class.

Grammar

Capitalizing Proper Nouns

Common nouns name a general person, place, or thing. They are only capitalized at the beginning of a sentence or in a title:

- Dogs are fun to play with.
- I read the book *Go, Dog, Go!* to my sister.

The pronoun *I* is always capitalized in a sentence.

Proper nouns name a specific person, place, or thing. They begin with a capital letter to set them apart from common nouns.

Names and titles of specific people
> **Max, Mr. Smith, President Washington**

Names of specific places
> **Australia, Maine, Chicago Public Library**

Names of specific things
> **Chicago Bears, Opal Mining Company**

Days of the week and months (except seasons)
> **Monday, Tuesday, January, February, spring**

Historical events and documents
> **World War I, the Constitution**

Titles of books, stories, and essays (only important words)
> **Alice in Wonderland, "The Underground City"**

Languages, races, and nationalities
> **Spanish language, Thai people, American**

Practice

Rewrite the sentences below using correct capitalization.

Example: opals are  native to coober pedy.

Opals are native to Coober Pedy.

1. dr. and mrs. robinson were late on friday.

2. steven hasn't read <u>a wrinkle in time</u>.

3. diamond mining has become popular in canada.

4. tracy is studying about greek architecture in school.

5. A goal in yellowstone national park is to protect the **environment**.

Apply

Work with a partner. Ask and answer the questions below. Write the answers using correct capitalization. Then compare them with your partner.

Example: A: What is your favorite book?

B: My favorite book is <u>My Side of the Mountain</u>.

- What is your favorite book?
- Who is your favorite singer?
- Who is your favorite movie actor?
- What is your favorite month?
- What town were you born in?
- What place would you like to visit?
- What language would you like to learn?
- What country would you like to visit?

Grammar Check ✓

How do you tell the difference between a common noun and a proper noun?

162

Writing

Ongoing
Writing
Skills
Practice

Write to Classify

When you classify, you group different kinds of information about a subject into categories. In each paragraph, discuss one category of information at a time.

Writing Prompt

Write two paragraphs that classify information about an animal. Think about how to organize information into categories. Capitalize proper nouns correctly.

❶ Prewrite

Choose an animal. Think about how you will classify, or group, information about the animal. Then list the information about each category on a Three-Column Chart.

A student named Joyce listed her information in this chart:

Features	Flying Birds	Flightless Birds
Wings	Longer wings	Shorter wings
Number of feathers	Fewer feathers	More feathers
Shape of feathers	Different shapes	Same shapes
Examples	Owls	Ostriches

❷ Draft

Use your Three-Column Chart to help you write a first draft.
- Keep in mind your purpose for writing—to classify.
- Group each category of information in one paragraph.

❸ Revise

Read over your draft. Look for places where the information categories are not clear or your sentences are too long. Use the Writing Checklist to help you identify problems. Then revise your draft.

❹ Edit

Check your work for errors. Trade papers with a partner to get feedback. Use the Peer Review Checklist on page 402. Edit your final draft in response to feedback from your partner and your teacher.

❺ Publish

Prepare a clean copy of your final draft. Share your paragraph with the class. Save your work. You will need to refer to it in the Writing Workshop.

Here are Joyce's paragraphs:

Writing Checklist

Ideas

✓ I clearly grouped the different kinds of information.

Word Choice

✓ I used interesting vocabulary in my paragraph.

Conventions

✓ I capitalized proper nouns correctly.

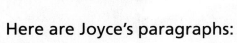

Joyce Lopez

While most birds fly, some birds can't fly. Flying birds have longer wings but fewer feathers. An owl is a flying bird that eats meat and hunts at night. Owls are found in North America and rain forests in South America.

Flightless birds first developed in islands. There they had few enemies to fly away from. These birds have shorter wings. They have more feathers all over their bodies. An ostrich is a fast-running, flightless bird that lives in Africa. These are the largest and heaviest of all birds.

163–164

Prepare to Read

What You Will Learn

Reading
- Vocabulary building: *Context, phonics*
- Reading strategy: *Identify author's purpose*
- Text type: *Literature (letters)*

Grammar
Prepositions and prepositional phrases

Writing
Organize ideas by problem and solution

These words will help you understand the reading.

Key Words

prairie

sod

climate

harsh

record

In *A House of Grass*, two cousins communicate through letters. One girl lives on the prairie. The other lives in a city.

Words in Context 🎧 Audio

1 In summer, the prairie is full of flowers and tall grasses.

2 Some people scatter grass seed and wait for the grass to grow. Others buy rolls of sod and have lawns right away.

3 The climate in this desert is harsh. It is always very dry. During the day, the desert gets very hot. At night, it gets very cold.

4 Our coach keeps a record of how many times we hit the ball.

Make flashcards to help you memorize the words.

- Write a key word on the front.

- On the back, write a sentence, but leave a blank where the key word should be.

Make Connections

Long ago, friends wrote letters to each other. How do friends communicate today? Which way do you like best? Why? Write your opinion in your notebook. Then explain it to a partner.

WB
165

These words will help you talk about the reading.

Academic Words

correspond
write and receive messages with someone

previously
before

reside
live somewhere

Academic Words

Words in Context

I **correspond** with my pen pal. He lives in Mexico.

Mr. Monroe **previously** worked in a bank. Now he is a famous writer.

All of my cousins **reside** in Phoenix.

Practice

Write the sentences in your notebook. Choose an academic word to complete each sentence.

1. Two friends might _____ in different cities, but they can still be good friends.

2. Now you can send messages through the phone. _____, this was not possible.

3. People can _____ using letters they send in the mail, or they can e-mail.

Apply

Ask and answer with a partner.

1. How would you **correspond** with friends who moved to a different city?

2. What is your favorite movie now? What was it **previously**?

3. How many people **reside** in your home?

Phonics

Y as a Vowel

Sometimes the letter *y* acts as a vowel. Each word in the chart below has the letter *y* at the end. Sound out the words.

- When does the letter *y* have the long /i/ sound?
- When does the letter *y* have the long /e/ sound?

Long /i/	Long /e/
by	city
dry	dirty
my	worry

Rule

- The letter *y* usually has the long /i/ sound when it comes after a consonant at the end of a one-syllable word.

- The letter *y* usually has the long /e/ sound when it comes after a consonant at the end of a word with more than one syllable.

Practice

Read the sentences with a partner. Take turns.

- Molly lives in the city.
- My new home is in Kansas.
- It was not easy to move.
- We share many stories.

1. List the words in which *y* has the long /i/ sound.
2. List the words in which *y* has the long /e/ sound.

167

LITERATURE
Letters

More About

In this selection, a young girl moves to a new home. Why does she **correspond** with her cousin back home?

Audio **Listen to the Audio.**
Listen for the main points and important details.

Reading Strategy

Identify Author's Purpose

Before you read, think about the author's purpose. Is the author writing:

- to entertain?
- to tell about something?
- to persuade you to do or think something?

As you read, think about why Sarah and Molly wrote their letters.

Listen as your teacher models the reading strategy.

A House of Grass

by Kathy Furgang

Dear Cousin Molly,

I often think of you, your nice home, and our beautiful Boston! The trip to Kansas has been long and hard. I look out the back of the wagon as the miles pass and I see only grass and more grass.

I have seen some funny houses on the prairie. They look like they are made of dirt. Ma says the prairie grass, or sod, is thick as a **mat**. She jokes that Pa will build us a sod house, too. It would be strange to live in a house made of dirt! How would we keep it clean?

Affectionately,
Sarah

---

mat   thick piece of material used to cover a floor

affectionately   way to end a letter, showing love or caring

Before You Go On   **Where did Sarah previously live?**

Dear Cousin Sarah,

I was happy to **receive** your letter. I hope you now have a nice new home. Please **assure** me it is not made of dirt! Mother said sod houses are hard to live in. They are tiny, their roofs leak, and the dirt walls are filled with bugs!

Will you ever return to Boston? The prairie must be a difficult place to live. Life is easier here.

I hope you keep a **diary**. If you keep a record of your adventures, one day your children can learn about your new life and experiences.

Love,
Molly

---

receive   get from someone

assure   tell or promise

diary   book in which you write things that happen each day

Reading Skill

If you don't understand something, ask your classmates or your teacher, "What does this mean?" If you are not sure, ask, "Does this mean...?"

Dear Molly,

I have funny news! We live in a sod house! It is dark and **damp,** but do not worry. It will protect us from the climate. It is an excellent shelter!

There are few trees on the prairie. The land looks like a sea of grass.

People here have little money, but they are **clever**. Since many can't buy wood, stone, or bricks, they build with sod. They cut the sod into pieces and then they **stack** the pieces like bricks to make things.

That is how Pa made our new house!

Love,
Sarah

---

damp   moist or a little bit wet

clever   creative and quick to learn

stack   form a neat pile of things, one on top of the other

Before You Go On   Why do people on the prairie reside in sod homes?

Dear Sarah,

I would love to live near you again, but I would not like to live on the **frontier**! I prefer my life in Boston.

When I look out my window, I see churches, museums, and stores. These are strong buildings that were built to last forever. But even rain could hurt your buildings. Your house could turn to mud.

A sod house does not **appeal** to me. I **certainly** do not like grass or dirt. I do not want to live with bugs!

I enjoy your letters. They help me learn about your new life.

Love,
Molly

---

frontier   area beyond places people know well

appeal   seem interesting or fun

certainly   without any doubt

Dear Molly,

Do not worry about me and my little sod house. I agree that sometimes the climate is harsh. But our house is cool in summer and warm in winter.

I love my new life on the prairie. I know that someday more people will move to the frontier and build towns and cities. Then we will have all the **comforts** of Boston!

Your loving cousin,
Sarah

168–170

comforts   things that make life nicer

Reading Strategy

Identify Author's Purpose

- Molly and Sarah had different reasons for **corresponding**. What were they?

- Did thinking about the author's purpose help you to understand the selection? How?

Think It Over

1. **Recall**   Why should Sarah keep a record of her adventures?

2. **Comprehend**   Where does Molly prefer to **reside**? Why?

3. **Analyze**   Would you like to live in a **sod** house? Why or why not?

Learning Strategies

Author's Purpose

Authors have different purposes for writing. An author writes to entertain, persuade, or inform. Knowing the author's purpose will help you understand what you read.

Read the sentences. Tell if the author's purpose is to entertain, persuade, or inform. Explain your answers.

1. Sod houses are made of dirt. Today's houses are made of brick or wood.

2. You will love our sod house. When it rains, the roof leaks. Then mud falls on your head!

3. Sod houses and today's houses protect you from harsh weather.

4. Sod houses are the best houses. They are cool in the summer and warm in the winter. You must build a sod house.

Use a Compare and Contrast Chart

A compare and contrast chart can help you compare
and contrast the information you are reading.

- When you **compare**, you tell how two or more things
  are alike.
- When you **contrast**, you tell how two or more things
  are different.

**Copy and complete this chart. Use the
questions below to help you.**

1. What other information from the
   selection can you put in the Alike box?

2. What other information from the
   selection can you put in the
   Different box?

3. What information from your own
   experiences can you put in the
   Alike box?

4. What information from your own
   experiences can you put in the Different box?

Sod Houses
and
Today's Houses

Alike

protect from
bad weather

Different

Sod: dirt

Today: brick
or wood

171

**Retell the selection to a partner. Use
academic and key words as you speak.**

Extension

Utilize Write a letter to Molly
or Sarah. Describe where you
live. Include a drawing that
shows some of what you are
describing. Share your drawing
with the class.

Grammar

Prepositions and Prepositional Phrases

A **preposition** is a word that shows location, time, direction, or provides details. Prepositions connect words in a sentence. Here are some common prepositions.

above	by	in	through
after	down	on	to
at	for	out	under
below	from	over	with

Prepositions are followed by a **noun** or **pronoun**. This is called a **prepositional phrase.** If the preposition explains *where* the cow jumped, then it is like an adverb because it describes the verb *jumped*.

> The cow *jumped* **over the moon.**

If a prepositional phrase describes a noun, then it is like an adjective.

> I like the *car* **with the white stripe.**

Prepositions can describe relationships with time.

> We will eat cake **after school.**

The first part of each sentence is a complete thought and can stand alone. The prepositional phrase is incomplete and depends on the rest of the sentence for its meaning.

Practice

Complete each sentence with a preposition.

Example: It was a harsh life <u>on</u> the prairie.

1. Do you live _____ an apartment or a house?

2. Are you _____ San Francisco?

3. Hector **resides** in the house _____ the tile roof.

4. The fox crawled _____ the tunnel.

5. **Previously**, he went _____ a private school.

Apply

Work with a partner. Discuss your hobbies and activities that you usually do on the weekend. Use prepositions and prepositional phrases.

Example: A: What do you like to do on the weekend?

B: I like to play with my dog in my yard.

- What do you like to do on the weekend?
- What time do you get up?
- Where do you like to go?
- How long have you liked this activity?
- Who goes with you?

Grammar Check ✔

What does a preposition tell us about a noun or verb?

172

Writing

Organize Ideas by Problem and Solution

Ongoing Writing Skills Practice

You can organize the ideas in your writing by describing problems and solutions. A problem is a difficulty that people face. A solution is the way to solve or fix the problem. First, describe the problem. Then, describe the solution.

Writing Prompt

Write a paragraph that describes a problem in your school or community. Then write a paragraph that explains how you solved it. Be sure to use prepositions correctly.

❶ Prewrite

Choose a problem to write about. Think about how you solved the problem. Then list the information in a problem and solution chart.

A student named Billy listed his ideas in this graphic organizer:

❷ Draft

Use your problem and solution chart to help you write a first draft.

PROBLEM	SOLUTION
Trash, bottles, and boxes filled the lot.	Students and teachers cleared out the lot.
No dirt to plant flowers and grass.	We carried bags of dirt and planted flowers and grass.
There were no lights or benches.	People gave money to buy lights and benches.

- Keep in mind your purpose for writing— to identity a problem and solution.

- Show clearly that each part of the problem has a solution.

❸ Revise

Read over your draft. Look for places where the writing is not well organized. Use the Writing Checklist to help you identify problems. Then revise your draft.

❹ Edit

Check your work for errors. Trade papers with a partner to get feedback. Use the Peer Review Checklist on page 402. Edit your final draft in response to feedback from your partner and your teacher.

❺ Publish

Prepare a clean copy of your final draft. Share your paragraph with the class. Save your work.

Writing Checklist

Ideas

✔ I clearly identified each problem and solution.

Organize

✔ I first wrote about the problems and then wrote the solutions.

Conventions

✔ I used prepositions correctly.

Here are Billy's paragraphs:

Billy Martin

I wanted to turn an empty lot near our school into a small community park. But the lot was filled trash, bottles, and boxes. There was no dirt to plant flowers and grass. There were no lights or benches, either. Without help, I wasn't sure how to make my dream come true.

My teacher, Ms. Han, told our school about the problem. Students and teachers worked together to clear out the lot. We planted flowers and grass. People gave us money. We used it to buy lights and benches. By working together we turned an empty lot into a beautiful park.

173–174

Prepare to Read

What You Will Learn

Reading

- Vocabulary building: *Context, phonics*

- Reading strategy: *Visualize*

- Text type: *Informational text (biography)*

Grammar
Present perfect

Writing
Write to compare and contrast

These words will help you understand the reading.

Key Words

pioneer

homestead

settler

orchard

chapel

Key Words

Words in Context

1 In the early history of the United States, many pioneer families moved west.

2 Families would build a small house, and they would farm the land on their new homestead.

3 An early settler had to work long hard hours to grow his own food and build his own place to live.

4 We have a small apple orchard in our town, where people can go to pick apples in the fall.

5 The chapel, or small church, was built many years ago. Now it is a historic place where tourists come to visit.

Practice

Draw a picture of a home that might be found during the pioneer days. Label the picture with sentences using key words.

Make Connections

What stories have you heard about pioneer men and women? Do you think you would have liked living during that time? Write your opinion in your notebook. Then explain it to a partner.

175

These words will help you talk about the reading.

Academic Words

Academic Words

considerable
large enough to be important

labor
hard work

undertake
take on as a responsibility

Words in Context

Ramona did a **considerable** amount of work on the group project.

Cleaning up the park involved a lot of physical **labor**.

The boys agreed to **undertake** the job of cleaning the garage.

Practice

Write the sentences in your notebook. Choose an academic word to complete each sentence.

1. Kenji chose to _____ the job of washing the dishes tonight.

2. Nina could not go to out to play because she had a _____ amount of homework.

3. Tony did not mind the _____ involved in raking leaves. He liked to work outside.

Apply

Ask and answer with a partner.

1. When did you have to **undertake** a tough job?

2. What kind of **labor** did you do?

3. Did the job take a **considerable** amount of time?

Phonics

R-Controlled Vowels: *ar, or, ore*

Listen. Then read each pair of words. Notice how the letter *r* changes the vowel sound.

am	ton	toe
arm	torn	tore

Here are more words with an *r* that follows a vowel. Sound out the words in the box.

art	for
hard	orchard
garden	more

Rule

The letters *ar* usually have the vowel sound heard in **art**. The letters *or* and *ore* usually have the vowel sound in **torn** and **tore**.

Practice

Read each pair of words with a partner. Tell whether the words have the same vowel sound.

1. bark, yard
2. port, park
3. part, pat
4. hose, horse

177

INFORMATIONAL TEXT
Biography

More About

What is it like to live in a one-room log house?

 Listen to the Audio.
Listen for the main points and important details.

Reading Strategy

Visualize

Readers often try to visualize, or see in their minds, what they are reading about.

- As you read, look for words that describe people, places, and things.
- Use the descriptions in the selection and the photos to help you create pictures in your mind.

Listen as your teacher models the reading strategy.

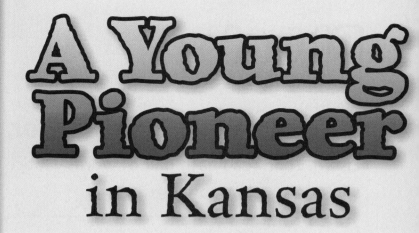

A Young Pioneer
in Kansas

by Barbara Davis

Have you heard the story of Mrs. Miriam D. Colt? She was a pioneer woman. As a young wife and mother, she lived the life of a settler. In April of 1856, Miriam and her family set out on a train from New York. They traveled with some other families who hoped to build a new life in the Kansas Territory.

After a few weeks and a **stopover** in Indiana, the Colts arrived in Kansas City, Missouri. They loaded all of their belongings into a covered wagon. Over the next few weeks, oxen pulled the wagons through rivers and across the prairie. Miriam had never seen such wide open spaces.

---

stopover a short stop during a trip to visit people or rest and eat

The Colts and the other families arrived at a place near the Neosho River. This is where the Colts hoped to build their homestead. They also hoped to build a small chapel.

At first, everyone lived in tents or in their wagons. It was hard to stay warm and dry. The spring weather had brought heavy rains that flooded the river. Strong winds howled across the prairie day and night. It was a wonder that the fruit trees Miriam had brought to plant in a new orchard didn't get blown away. She would have been **heartbroken** had she lost the little trees.

---

heartbroken filled with grief and sorrow

Reading Skill

Ask your teacher or classmates when you don't understand a word, phrase, or language structure.

The Kansas Territory was created as part of the Kansas-Nebraska Act of 1854. The open land made it attractive to many settlers looking for cheap farmland or cattle-grazing areas.

Before You Go On   Why did the Colts **undertake** this journey?

There was a small cabin on the property that the Colts hoped to settle. As soon as he could, Mr. Colt got to work to make it a comfortable home. He smoothed the dirt floor in the cabin and put in flat stones. He built shelves to hold the family's tin cups and dishes.

For their bedding, Miriam filled large, cotton bags with dried prairie grass. Round pieces of logs served as table tops. The trunks in which the Colts had brought their clothes were used as chairs. Bags of flour and cornmeal were stored in a corner. The whole family slept and ate in one room. It was too small for a cooking fire, so Miriam cooked outside.

Although the days were filled with work, the Colt family also had time for fun. Miriam and her children gathered flowers from the prairie. The children ran through the grass and played games. Miriam warned them to keep a sharp eye out for rattlesnakes that lived on the prairie. The children already knew to stay away from skunks!

The rains and winds of spring finally passed. Miriam and her family enjoyed the warm, sunny summer days. The fields were full of healthy crops. Miriam was amazed at how easy it was to grow beans, pumpkins, melons, potatoes, and corn.

The ability to grow plenty of food was important to pioneer families. There were no stores to buy food, clothing, or furniture. They had to do everything for themselves. Pioneers learned to value simple things. Pioneers like the Colt family and their neighbors thought of **clever** ways to use common objects for useful purposes. Bits of cloth could be sewn together to make a blanket or a doll. String could be used as a wick in a candle or knotted for a fishing line.

Pioneers faced many challenges in their **quest** for a better life. They are heroes in their own ways because they bravely faced these challenges to build a new future.

Pioneers tried hard not to waste anything. Scraps of cloth, bits of yarn, and other things we might consider useless were put to good use.

---

clever smart and quick-thinking

quest long search

Reading Strategy

Visualize

- What did you visualize as you read about the Colts' one-room house?
- What did you visualize as read about the spring wind and rain Miriam and her family experienced?
- Did visualizing help you understand the selection? How?

Think It Over

1. **Recall** What does Miriam notice about the crops?

2. **Comprehend** What are some **considerable** hardships that the Colts faced?

3. **Analyze** What types of **labor** might Miriam's children have done as part of their daily chores?

Learning Strategies

Visualize

When you read, try to **visualize**, or picture in your mind, what the author is describing. Authors use words to help readers create mind pictures.

Practice

What picture do you visualize when you read each sentence? Choose one sentence and draw what you visualize.

1. People can make tree houses in backyards. They must secure wooden boards to strong tree branches.
2. Some people build tree houses high in the jungle.
3. Some tree houses have many rooms. They even have staircases.
4. People who live in tree houses nest high in the sky with the birds.

Use an Organizational Chart

Your organizational chart helps you put your thoughts in order. Suppose you want a friend to picture the different places that Miriam Colt and her family traveled to. The chart will help you think of ways to describe the different scenes.

 **Practice**

Copy and complete this chart. Then answer the questions.

Scenes of Places Traveled	Object Described	Detail 1	Detail 2
Colts traveling to Kansas Territory as pioneers	wagon	pulled by oxen	Had all of the family's belongings

1. Describe to a partner the scenes from the selection you added to your chart. Use a **considerable** amount of detail in your description.

2. How did the organizational chart help you describe the scene?

3. What did the Colts do to make their homestead a more comfortable place to live?

181

4. Would you have wanted to be a settler in the Kansas Territory during this period? Why or why not?

 **Apply**

Using the pictures, summarize the story for a partner.

Extension

Utilize Suppose you could undertake the designing of your own homestead. Draw or describe it. Share your design with your class.

Grammar

Present Perfect

The **present perfect tense** is often used to talk about experiences that happened in the past. The exact time isn't mentioned because you are talking about a broad period of time.

> **Have** you ever **been** to New York?
>
> Yes, I **have**. I**'ve been** there once.

The present perfect is formed with *have* and the **past participle**. You can use a **contraction** for *have* or *has*.

> He **has studied** karate **before**.

> **have = 've   has = 's**

You can form most past participles by adding *-ed* to the verb, but some past participles are irregular.

> | | | |
> |---|---|---|
> | be → been | get → gotten | see → seen |
> | eat → eaten | meet → met | spend → spent |
> | fly → flown | ride → ridden | write → written |

Use the present prefect with non-specific time phrases such as *once, ever, never, before*, or *a few times*. To talk about a specific event, use the simple past.

Present Perfect	Simple Past
I**'ve been** to New York before.	I **went** there **last summer.**

Use the present perfect tense of each verb.
Write the sentences.

Example: They <u>have visited</u> the apple
orchard. (visit)

1. We _____ to Oregon. (be)

2. She _____ a book about settlers. (write)

3. I _____ a **considerable** amount of time on my
   homework. (spend)

4. The mayor _____ pioneers to settle the town. (welcome)

5. The students _____ for a quiet room to work in. (look)

Apply

Work with a partner. Use the prompts below to ask and
answer questions. Try to use the present perfect tense.

Example: A: Have you ever been to California?

B: Yes, I have. I have been there a few times.

- been to
  California?
- ridden a horse?
- flown on
  an airplane?
- met a famous
  person?

- visited a
  national park?
- eaten sushi?
- seen a horror
  movie?
- gotten a very
  bad present?

**Grammar
Check** ✔

When do we use the
present perfect?

182

Writing

Write to Compare and Contrast

Ongoing Writing Skills Practice

When you compare two things you explain how they are alike.
When you contrast two things you explain how they are different.
Use details to show how the things are alike and different.

Writing Prompt

Write a paragraph to compare and contrast two sports or hobbies.
Use details to show how they are alike and different. Be sure to
use present perfect verbs correctly.

❶ Prewrite

G.O. 142

Choose two sports or
hobbies to compare
and contrast. Think
about how they are
alike and different.
Then list your ideas
in a Venn Diagram.

A student named Julie
listed her ideas like this.

Baseball

• Players use a glove and a bat.

• Players take turns.

• Sometimes, players must wait a long time.

Both

sports are fun.

Soccer

• You kick the ball with your feet.

• Players run all the time.

• There's lots of activity for every player.

❷ Draft

Use your Venn Diagram to help you write a first draft.

• Keep in mind your purpose for writing—to compare and contrast.
• Include details that show how the sports are alike and different.

❸ Revise

Read over your draft. Look for places where the writing is unclear. Use the Writing Checklist to help you identify problems. Then revise your draft.

❹ Edit

Check your work for errors. Trade papers with a partner to get feedback. Use the Peer Review Checklist on page 402. Edit your final draft in response to feedback from your partner.

❺ Publish

Prepare a clean copy of your final draft. Share your paragraph with the class. Save your work.

Here is Julie's compare and contrast paragraph:

Writing Checklist

Ideas

✓ I showed how the subjects are alike and different.

Word Choice

✓ I used details to compare and contrast.

✓ I used irregular past verbs correctly.

Julie Fernandez

Baseball and soccer are both fun sports to play, but they are very different. In baseball, you catch a ball with a glove and hit it with a bat. In soccer, you kick the ball with your feet. You can use your head, too, but not your hands. In baseball, players take turns batting and running to the bases. Sometimes they wait a long time. In soccer, players run all the time. I have played soccer for two years, while my brother has played baseball. I like soccer better because there is more activity for every player.

183–184

Apply and Extend

Link the Readings

Copy the chart into your notebook. Read the words in the top row. Then follow these steps:

- For *The Underground City*, put an X under the words that remind you of the text.
- Repeat the same activity *for A House of Grass* and *A Young Pioneer in Kansas*.

	Informational text	Literature	Hard Times	Harsh Climate
The Underground City				
A House of Grass				
A Young Pioneer in Kansas				

Discussion

1. Why are the people of Coober Pedy happy about where they **reside**?

2. How does Sarah think life on the prairie will change in the future?

3. The people in *A House of Grass* and *A Young Pioneer in Kansas* talk about their new neighbors. How are the neighbors similar?

What is it like to live in an unusual home?

> **Listening Skills**
>
> If you don't understand something a speaker says, you can say, "I don't understand. Can you explain it, please?"

Projects

Your teacher will help you choose one of these projects.

Written	**Oral**	**Visual/Active**
Journal Entry	**Description**	**Illustration**
Imagine you live in one of the houses you read about. Write a journal entry describing a day in your life. Include specific details and descriptions.	Describe one of the houses you read about. Give details, but do not identify the house. Have listeners guess which house you are describing.	Choose one of the houses you read about. Create your own illustration of that house. Use the illustrations in the book as a guide.
Building Proposal	**Interview**	**Charades**
Think of a new kind of house. Write a proposal for building that house. Tell why your house would be special. Include details.	Interview someone who lives in a different kind of house than you. Ask about the good and bad parts of living in that house. Record your interview.	Choose a house you read about. Act out a daily activity in that house. Have other students guess which house you are living in. Act out living in other houses.

Further Reading

 For more projects visit
LongmanCornerstone.com

 Pinocchio
The theme of this Penguin Young Reader® folktale—wanting to belong—is universal. A wooden boy wishes to be a real boy and to have a real home.

Prairie Town, Bonnie Geisert
Life in an early twentieth-century midwestern prairie town is shown through seasonal events, such as plowing, planting, harvest time, and winter blizzards.

185–186

Listening and Speaking Workshop

Present a TV Talk Show

You are going to write and present a TV talk show. Then you will listen as your classmates present a TV talk show, too.

❶ Prepare

A. Find two partners. One will be the host, and the other two will be the guests. Your group will present a TV talk show about where people live. Your classmates (the audience) will ask the guests questions at the end of the show.

B. Choose two interesting places where people live. Do some research for facts, details, and examples. Share the information and work cooperatively. Then write your TV talk show. Find photos or simple props to show during the talk show.

Host:	Welcome to our show today. We have two special guests. Maria and Tobias. Let's have each of you tell our audience where you live. Maria?
Maria:	I live in a cave.
Host:	And, Tobias, what about you?
Tobias:	I live on a boat.
Host:	Two very different places, two very different homes. Maria, where is your cave. . . I mean home?

❷ Practice

Practice your TV talk show with your props in front of your family or friends. If possible, record your talk show. Then listen to it. Record it again and try to improve.

❸ Present

As you speak, do the following:
- Speak loudly and face your audience.
- Use hand and body movements to make a point.
- Answer your audience's questions.

As you listen, do the following:
- Think about what you already know about the subject.
- If you don't understand something, you can say, "Excuse me. Could you repeat that, please?"
- Think of questions to ask at the end of the talk show.

❹ Evaluate

After you speak, answer these questions:
- ✓ Did you speak loudly and face your audience?
- ✓ Did you give interesting facts, details, and examples in your answers?

After you listen, answer these questions:
- ✓ Did you understand the questions and answers?
- ✓ Did you ask a question?
- ✓ Did you enjoy the talk show?

> **Speaking Skills**
>
> Choose your words based on who is listening. A TV talk show is informal. Use simple, conversational language.

> **Listening Skills**
>
> Listen carefully for specific facts and observations to predict what you don't already know.
>
> Listen carefully for ideas and information that aren't stated directly.

Writing Workshop

Write a Magazine or Newspaper Article

Writing Prompt

Write a magazine or newspaper article about something that happened in your school or community. Answer each of the 5W questions: Who? What? Where? When? and Why?

❶ Prewrite

Review your previous work in this unit. Then choose a topic. Think about something that happened recently in your school or community. Research information about the event that answers the 5W questions. List your ideas in a graphic organizer.

A student named Rosie listed her ideas on this chart:

> WHO?: _____
> Ms. Irene Gomez

> WHAT?: _____
> Hampton Community Center opened

> WHERE?: _____
> three blocks from our school

> WHEN?: _____
> October 1

> WHY?: _____
> offers many services, including classes, for our community

❷ Draft

Use your graphic organizer to write a draft.

- Keep your purpose in mind—to write a magazine or newspaper article.
- Research information to answer the 5W questions.

❸ Revise

Read over your draft. Look for places where the writing needs improvement. Use the Writing Checklist to help you. Then revise your draft. Here is how Rosie revised her newspaper article:

Six Traits of Writing Checklist

✔ **Ideas**
Did I write about something in my school or community?

✔ **Organization**
Do I answer the 5W questions?

✔ **Voice**
Is my tone serious?

✔ **Word Choice**
Did I choose precise words?

✔ **Sentence Fluency**
Did I use different sentence types?

✔ **Conventions**
Did I spell homophones correctly?

Rosie Humphrey

Hampton Community Center Opens

Philadelphia, PA, October 10

The Hampton Community Center opened October 1, just three blocks from our school. Last week Ms. Irene Gomez, the director, gave me a guided tour.

> **Revised** to correct mechanical error.

The center offers many services, including classes, for members of our community. Currently, there are eight classrooms for adults and children. The courses range from cooking and welding to drawing and job training. and resume writing classes help prepare adults and teens to find work.

> **Revised** to create a sentence.

Ms. Gomez said a new indoor pool will be ready by next summer. Free swimming classes will be offered every morning of the week. To enroll, you must fill out an application form by June 1.

> **Revised** to correct spelling error.

Future plans for the center include movie nights, concerts, and art events. Ms. Gomez believes the community center will help all of us. She encourages everyone in our school to visit soon.

> **Revised** to make meaning clearer.

④ Edit

Check your work for errors. Trade papers with a partner. Use the Peer Review Checklist to give each other feedback.

⑤ Publish

Prepare a clean copy of your final draft. Share your essay with the class.

187–188

Peer Review Checklist

✓ The article answers all 5W questions.

✓ The writing is informative.

✓ The main ideas and details are clearly organized.

SPELLING TIP

Homophones are words that sound alike, but are spelled differently and have different meanings.

Example: patients/patience

Use a dictionary to check the spelling of homophones.

Listen to the sentences. Pay attention to the groups of words. Read aloud.

1. Many visitors come to see the underground architecture in Coober Pedy, Australia.

2. Molly's letters to her cousin Sarah describe life in a sod house on the Kansas prairie.

3. Mrs. Miriam Colt was a pioneer woman who faced hardships and challenges when she settled in the Kansas Territory in the 1850s.

Work in pairs. Take turns reading the passage aloud for one minute. Count the number of words you read.

Have you ever seen an underground house? Come visit	9
a town called Coober Pedy!	14
About 3,500 people live in Coober Pedy, Australia.	22
From the street, you might see only dirt and some	32
trees. But underground, there are homes! More	39
than half of the people in the town live in	49
underground houses. These are regular houses that	56
look a lot like yours!	61
The summer heat in Coober Pedy is extreme, but the	71
underground homes are efficient. They stay cool	78
during the hot months. That means people don't spend	87
money on air conditioning. In the winter, the homes	96
stay warm, and that means people pay less for heat.	106
When opal mining became popular in Coober Pedy,	114
miners noticed the cool air in the mines. That's how	124
the underground homes began.	128

With your partner, find the words that slowed you down.

- Practice saying each word and then say the sentence each word is in.

189–190

- Then take turns reading the text again. Count the number of words you read.

Test Preparation

Taking Tests

You will often take tests that help show what you know. Follow these tips to improve your test-taking skills.

Coaching Corner

Answering Questions About a Selection

- Many test questions have you answer questions about a selection.

- The selection can be fiction or nonfiction.

- Before you read the selection, preview the questions and answer choices.

- Look for words like *best, least, main, most, most likely, not,* and *probably.*

- After reading the selection, first try to answer each question in your head.

- Choose the answer that comes closest to the answer in your head.

- Make sure your answer choice is supported by the text.

Read the following test sample. Study the tips in the box.

191–192

Read the selection. Then answer the questions.

Prairie Dogs

1   A prairie dog is a rodent that is about the size of a rabbit. Prairie dogs are very social animals. Many species live together underground in large networks of burrows called towns. The towns can cover one half of a square mile and house hundreds of animals. The towns have special rooms where prairie dogs store food and raise their young.

2   Prairie dogs may share their burrows with other animals such as snakes, burrowing owls, and ferrets. They feed on grass during the day. They guard the entrances to their towns. If a predator comes, the guard prairie dog barks to warn the others.

1 Where are many prairie dogs most likely to live?

   A In underground burrows

   B On hilltops

   C With rabbits

   D In Arctic towns

2 In paragraph 1, <u>social</u> means —

   F liking to be with others

   G living in tiny burrows

   H a friendly gathering

   J predatory

3 What is one way in which prairie dogs protect one another?

   A They store food and raise their young.

   B They gather grass for all of them to eat.

   C They share their homes with rabbits.

   D They guard the entrances to their towns.

Tips

✔ Read the question and answer choices before you read the selection.

✔ Sometimes you can infer something to help you answer test questions. What can you infer from the last two sentences?

Links to Our Past

Do you ever think about the past? Stories about the past can help you learn about or remember life long ago.

Reading

1 Short Story	2 Short Story	3 Social Studies

The Moon Tree	**A Hike Back in Time**	**The History of Money**

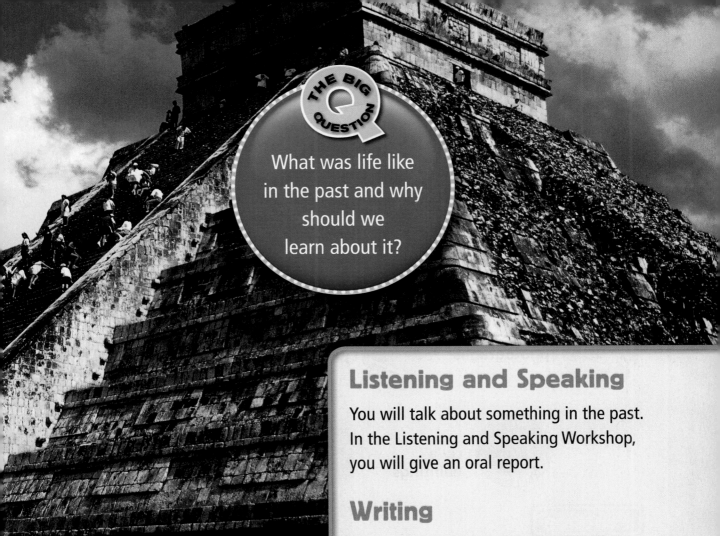

What was life like in the past and why should we learn about it?

Listening and Speaking

You will talk about something in the past. In the Listening and Speaking Workshop, you will give an oral report.

Writing

You will practice skills needed to write a research report. In the Writing Workshop, you will write a research report.

Quick Write

Does your family tell stories from the past? Describe an interesting or exciting event from your family's past.

VIEW AND RESPOND

Talk about the poster for this unit. Then watch and listen to the video and answer the questions at LongmanCornerstone.com.

What do you know about the past?

Words to Know

Listen and repeat. Use these words to talk about studying the past.

 photographs

 journals

 museums

 cave paintings

 fossils

Practice

Work with a partner. Ask and answer questions using the words above, from the box, or your own ideas.

read	study	visit	look at

Example: A: How can you learn about the past?

B: I can <u>study</u> <u>cave paintings</u>.

Write

Read the questions. Write your response in your notebook.

What are some events in your life that you would like to remember in the future? What could you do to remember them?

Make Connections

Copy the sentences below into your notebook. Complete the sentences with the following words.

what people wore

prehistoric animals

prehistoric people

what people did

1. We can learn a lot by studying cave paintings. One way _____ communicated was through art.

2. Carlos and his brothers like to look at the fossils of _____ at the Field Museum in Chicago.

3. By reading journals from long ago you could find out what games people played and _____ to have fun.

4. I love to look at my grandparents' photo albums to see what people looked like and _____ when they were my age.

What about you?

Talk with a partner. How do you save special memories?

Kids' Stories from around the World 🔊 Audio

France

India

Marie-Paule

I live in France. I like to visit caves where people lived long ago. You can see tools and clothing that prehistoric people used. Many of the caves have paintings on the walls. Ancient people painted objects and animals that were important to them.

Rajan

I live in India. There are many weavers in my country. They use colorful wool yarns to make beautiful fabric. Many of the patterns are hundreds of years old. They have been passed down through generations.

Washington, D.C. U.S.A.

Mexico

Jacob

I live in Washington, D.C. That is the capital of the United States. My mom works for the United States Mint. That is where American money is printed. Mom says we can learn a lot about a country's past by looking at its money. George Washington's picture is on our dollar bill. He was our first president.

Alicia

I live in Mexico. My favorite day is September 16th. That is the day Mexico became free from Spain. Every year, my country celebrates its birthday. We dress in special clothes on that day. We also sing special songs that celebrate our past.

What about you?

1. What object would you like to save to help you remember your past? Why?

2. What are some ways that your family celebrates the past? Describe them. Share your story.

What You Will Learn

Reading

- Vocabulary building: *Context, phonics*

- Reading strategy: *Identify problem and solution*

- Text type: *Literature (short story)*

Grammar

Compound sentences: *and, but, or*

Writing

Plan a research report

These words will help you understand the reading.

Key Words

signatures

mission

astronaut

plaque

explorer

surrounded

Key Words

The Moon Tree tells about two boys who try to save an important tree.

Words in Context

1 Some people wanted a park in the city. They asked everyone to sign a form. They needed as many **signatures** as possible.

2 The *Apollo 11* space **mission** was the first time a human landed on the moon. Scientists worked for many years to make the mission a success.

3 An **astronaut** must wear a spacesuit to go outside of the space shuttle.

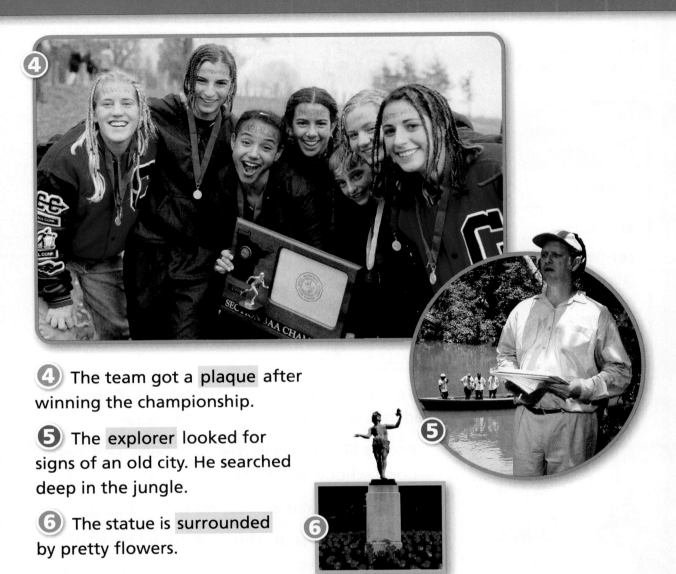

4 The team got a plaque after winning the championship.

5 The explorer looked for signs of an old city. He searched deep in the jungle.

6 The statue is surrounded by pretty flowers.

Practice

Make flashcards to help you memorize the words.
- Write a key word on the front.
- On the back, write the meaning.

Make Connections

Some buildings have plaques telling about a famous person who lived there. Imagine a plaque on the place where you live. What would it say about you? After discussing this question, write your response in your notebook using the key words.

193

These words will help you talk about the reading.

Academic Words

achieve
succeed in doing something

community
group of people who live in the same area

unique
special, one of a kind

Academic Words

Words in Context

With hard work and practice, Tom was able to **achieve** his goal of learning to play the guitar.

Our **community** all worked together to get more books for our town library.

Your presentation was **unique** because no one else in the class did that.

Practice

Write the sentences in your notebook. Choose an academic word to complete each sentence.

1. People like to live in this _____ because it has good schools and libraries.

2. Every snowflake is _____, no two are alike.

3. To _____ success in school you need to work hard and do your homework.

Apply

Ask and answer with a partner.

1. What would you like to **achieve** by next year?

2. What makes a good **community**?

3. What makes you **unique**?

194

Phonics

Diphthongs: *ow, ou*

Listen as your teacher reads the words.
Notice the vowel sounds in these words.
Then read the words aloud.

> how　　loud　　low

Which words have the same letters?
Which words have the same vowel sound?

Rule

The letters *ow* and *ou* can have the vowel sound you hear in **how** and **loud**. The letters *ow* can also have the long o sound you hear in **low**. The words **how** and **low** have the same *ow* spelling, but different sounds.

Practice

Read the words below with a partner.

> around　　cow　　show
>
> down　　know　　south
>
> flower　　out　　tomorrow

- List the words in which *ow* has the long o sound in **low**.
- List the words in which *ow* or *ou* has the vowel sound in **how**.

LITERATURE
Short Story

More About

Why is it important for people to save things from the past?

Audio **Listen to the Audio.**
First, listen for the main points. Then listen again for the important details. Take notes as you listen. Retell the story to a partner.

Reading Strategy

Identify Problem and Solution

- As you read, think about the problems the characters face.
- Keep reading to find the solutions to the problems.
- Ask your teacher or classmates if you don't understand.

Listen as your teacher models the reading strategy.

The Moon Tree

by Dan Ahearn
illustrated by Lee White

The ball flew like a rocket into the woods. Hector found the ball next to a strange, flat stone that was dirty and scratched. It rested against a tall **sycamore** tree. On the stone was a brass plaque . It said:

> *The seed of this tree was a space explorer .*
> *It went to the moon*
> *with the **crew** of the **Apollo 14**.*
> *The seed was planted here on July 4, 1976.*

Hector ran to get his friend Stuart. He didn't notice the red flags that circled the tree.

---

sycamore   North American tree with broad leaves

crew   people who work together

Apollo 14   third spaceship to land on the moon

Before You Go On   What did Hector find when he was looking for a ball?

Hector and Stuart ran to the library, and they read about the moon trees. The boys learned that 500 seeds went on the space mission. The seeds didn't land on the moon. They stayed in **orbit** with astronaut Stuart Roosa. It had been his idea to bring the seeds.

Back on Earth, the seeds grew into normal trees. Space travel had not changed them. People planted hundreds of moon tree **seedlings**, and the trees grew all over the world.

The boys told the librarian, Mrs. Wu, about the moon tree.

---

orbit   a path in space made when one thing moves around a larger thing

seedlings   young plants grown from seeds

Fig. 1 - APOLLO

"I forgot about our moon tree," said Mrs. Wu. "But I have bad news." She explained that most of the woods would be gone soon. **Stakes** with red flags surrounded each tree that would be cut down.

"Why?" cried Hector.

"To make room for the new shopping mall," said Mrs. Wu.

"That's not right," said Stuart. "There must be something we can do!"

Mrs. Wu said they needed a plan. She and the boys talked all day about how to save the moon tree. By the time the library closed, they had a plan.

---

stakes pointed objects stuck in the ground to mark places

Before You Go On   What problem did the boys discover?

The boys met with their friends. They told their friends the plan to save the moon tree.

Hector held up a paper. "This is a **petition**," he said. "It says, 'The moon tree is an important part of history. It is too valuable to lose. Please **spare** our moon tree.' We need everybody in town to sign this petition."

"Signatures will show that people care," Stuart said. "We need a lot of signatures. Then the builders might not cut down the moon tree."

Hector said, "Ask everybody to sign the petition! Save the moon tree!"

---

petition   written request signed by a lot of people

spare   save or not damage

They called themselves the Moon Tree Crew. Then Stuart named the tree. He said, "Our moon tree needs a name. People will care more about a tree called . . . Apollo."

Stuart knew about these things. His father worked in the **advertising** business.

Mrs. Wu made posters. Each poster had a **slogan**, "Save Apollo, the moon tree."

The boys and their friends were busy. Some went to stores, others walked down Main Street. They told people the moon tree's story. The whole town wanted to help so the Moon Tree Crew got hundreds of signatures.

---

advertising business that tells people about a product

slogan short phrase that is easy to remember

Before You Go On How did the **community** become involved?

Hector and Stuart took the petition to Mr. Bowman. He built shopping malls for a **living**.

"Boys, you've made this tree famous," he said. "How did you do it?"

"My father told me how," said Stuart. "He works in advertising."

Mr. Bowman laughed. "When I was your age, I saw the first **lunar** landing on TV. But has this tree really been to the moon?"

"Yes, but it was only a seed then," said Hector.

"It never actually landed on the moon," Stuart added. "It only **orbited** the moon."

Mr. Bowman was silent for a moment. "That's close enough for me," he said.

---

living   way to earn money

lunar   about the moon

orbited   traveled in a circle in space around a larger thing

Mr. Bowman did build a shopping mall, but he saved Apollo, the moon tree. He had the old plaque cleaned and shined. Under the old plaque, he added a new one. It said:

The Moon Tree Crew saved this tree.

"Thank you!" said Hector and Stuart.

"No, thank you," said Mr. Bowman. "This tree brings all of us closer to the moon."

196–198

Reading Strategy

Identify Problem and Solution

- What problems did the boys in the story have?
- How did they solve the problems?
- Did thinking about the problems and solutions help you understand this story? How?

Think It Over

1. **Recall** What was **unique** about the moon tree?

2. **Comprehend** Why was the moon tree in danger? Explain.

3. **Analyze** How did the boys **achieve** their goal?

Learning Strategies

Problem and Solution

Problems and solutions make a story more interesting. A **problem** is a conflict that characters have. The **solution** is how characters solve, or fix, the problem. There can be more than one problem and solution in a story.

As you read, ask yourself:

- "What is the main, or most important, conflict?"
- "What does the main character want?"

 **Practice**

Write the solution to each problem. The first one is done for you.

PROBLEM	SOLUTION
1. Hector and Stuart wanted to learn about moon trees.	1. Hector and Stuart went to the library to read about moon trees.
2. Hector, Stuart, and Mrs. Wu wanted to save the **unique** tree.	2.
3. Hector, Stuart, and Mrs. Wu wanted the **community** to know about their plan.	3.
4. Mr. Bowman wanted to build a new shopping mall.	4.

Use a Problem and Solution Chart

A Problem and Solution Chart can help you record problems
and solutions in a story.

Practice

Copy this chart. Then reread *The Moon Tree*.
Write about the main problem and its solution.

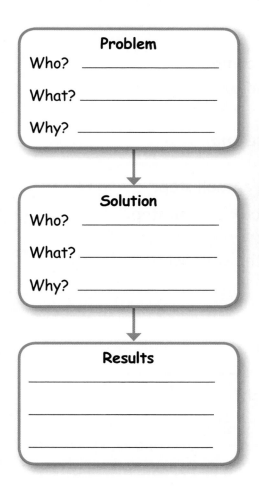

Problem
Who? _____
What? _____
Why? _____

Solution
Who? _____
What? _____
Why? _____

Results
_____
_____
_____

WB
199

Apply

Outline the events in the story. Then
narrate the story using key words.

Extension

Utilize   Work in small groups.
If you were with Hector and
Stuart, what would you have
done? Write a skit explaining
how you would have solved the
problem. As you work together,
listen to each other's ideas.
Present the skit to the class.

Grammar

Compound Sentences: *and, but, or*

A **simple sentence** has a subject and a verb. It forms a complete thought.

> The boys played baseball.

Two simple sentences can be joined to form a **compound sentence** using connecting words *and, but,* and *or*.

Compound sentence with *and*

To combine two similar sentences together, use *and*.

> The astronaut went to the moon. He took a small step.
>
> The astronaut went to the moon, **and** he took a small step.

- Remember to always use a comma before the connecting word in a compound sentence.

Compound sentence with *but*

To combine two contrasting sentences, use *but*.

> Tim wants to be a pilot. He is afraid of heights.
>
> Tim wants to be a pilot, **but** he is afraid of heights.

Compound sentence with *or*

To offer a choice, use *or* between two sentences.

> They can go out to eat. They can cook dinner at home.
>
> They can go out to eat, **or** they can cook dinner at home.

Practice

Use connecting words *and*, *but*, or *or* to combine the sentences.

Example: Many seeds went on the space mission.
The seeds didn't land on the moon.

Many seeds went on the space mission, but the seeds didn't land on the moon.

1. He finally **achieved** his dream. He failed the first time.

2. The painting could be an original. It could be a fake.

3. The signatures were collected. Then they turned in the petition.

4. The **community** voted for the law. No one obeyed it.

5. The explorer was brave. She took many chances.

Work with a partner. Read the sentences about *The Moon Tree*. Combine them using *and*, *but* or *or*. Then rewrite them.

Example: A: The moon tree grew in the woods.
It would soon be cut down.

B: The moon tree grew in the woods, but it would soon be cut down.

- The moon tree grew in the woods. It would soon be cut down.
- Mrs. Wu and the boys talked all day. They devised a plan.
- They made a petition. They needed a lot of signatures.
- Signatures could save the trees. Builders could cut them down.

200

Grammar Check ✔

How do you connect two sentences?

Writing

Plan a Research Report

Ongoing Writing Skills Practice

In a research report, you explain a topic that you have studied fully. You include information that you have gathered from different sources.

Choose a Topic

Before you can write a research report, you need to choose a topic. You can begin by thinking of a broad topic. Then ask yourself questions about this topic and do a little research. Your findings can give you ideas for a more specific topic. Then think of an open-ended question, which is a question that needs more than a one or two word response. This will be the topic of your report.

Task 1

Think about topic ideas, and ask yourself some questions. What interests you? What would you like to learn more about? List your ideas, questions, and answers in a graphic organizer.

A student named Jamie listed his ideas in this chart:

BROAD TOPIC:	The Fourth of July
QUESTION:	How do we celebrate the Fourth of July?
ANSWER:	We have picnics and parades and watch fireworks.
QUESTION:	Why is the Fourth of July also called Independence Day?
ANSWER:	On July 4, 1776, the Continental Congress adopted the Declaration of Independence.

The answer Jamie found to his question about why the Fourth of July is also called Independence Day helped him decide to write about the history of this American holiday.

Write a Research Question

Jamie still needed to write a question to direct his research. He made a list of open-ended questions about Independence Day.

1. What is the Declaration of Independence?
2. When and how did Americans celebrate Independence Day ?
3. Do other countries celebrate Independence Day?

Task 2

Once you've narrowed your topic, write a list of open-ended questions. Then study the questions. Which one interests you the most? This question will direct the research for your report.

Make a Research Plan

Jamie chose question number 2 as the topic for his report. To create a research plan, he made a list of things he wanted to know about his topic. He listed them in a T-chart.

What do I want to know?	Where can I find it?
1. When and how did people celebrate the First Independence Day?	http://www.history.com/content/fourthofjuly/history—of—july—4th Book: Independence Day: Birthday of the United States by Elaine Landau
2. What was the history of this holiday after 1776?	http://www.pbs.org/capitolfourth/history.html
3. How do Americans celebrate Independence Day in their communities today?	Encyclopedia: World Book Encyclopedia, article by Theodore Hershberg

Task 3

Finally, create a research plan. Make a list of what you want to learn and where to look for it. Use a T-chart like the above.

201–202

What You Will Learn

- Vocabulary building: *Context, phonics*
- Reading strategy: *Identify plot and setting*
- Text type: *Literature (short story)*

Grammar
Past progressive

Writing
Paraphrasing a source

These words will help you understand the reading.

Key Words

thrive

hiking

trails

thrilling

canyon

ledge

Key Words

A Hike Back in Time is a story about a girl who visits the Grand Canyon.

Words in Context

1 Plants need water to grow and thrive . Which plant do you think gets more water?

2 Hiking is a lot of fun. You don't need a bike or a car. You just walk on trails that go up a mountain.

③ The rides at the fair are thrilling! They are scary and fun at the same time.

④ The canyon was deep and wide.

⑤ The hiker stopped to look over the ledge of the mountain.

 **Practice**

Add a page to your vocabulary notebook.

- Divide your page into three columns: the new words, their definitions, and a sentence using the new word.

- Test yourself by covering one of the columns.

Make Connections

Have you ever been on a hike? Where did you go? If you have not been on a hike, where would you like to go? Why? Be sure to use key words as you speak.

203

These words will help you talk about the reading.

Academic Words

equipped
provided with things that are needed to do something

motivated
determined or eager to do something

route
way from one place to another

Academic Words

Words in Context

When you go hiking, it is important that you are **equipped** with good hiking boots.

Emily was **motivated** to finish her homework quickly because she wanted to go outside and play.

The map shows the best **route** to school.

Practice

Write the sentences in your notebook. Choose an academic word to complete each sentence.

1. The _____ I take to my friend's house goes through the park.

2. I was _____ with water and a hat for my hike.

3. I was _____ to read a lot of books so that I could win the award.

Apply

Ask and answer with a partner.

1. What does a well **equipped** student need?

2. What subject in school are you **motivated** to do well in?

3. What is the best **route** from your house to school?

Phonics

Variant Vowel: *oo*

Listen as your teacher reads the words in the chart. Identify the two sounds of the letters *oo*. Then read the words aloud.

Words with Letters *oo*	
book	too
wood	proof
foot	room

Rule

Sometimes the letters *oo* have the sound you hear in **took**.
Sometimes the letters *oo* have the sound you hear in **soon**.

Practice

Read the sentences with a partner. Take turns.

- Come look at my scrapbook.
- It has pictures of the trip we took.
- We spent the afternoon walking in the woods.
- There's a pool near the waterfall.

  1. List the words in which *oo* has the vowel sound in *took*.

  2. List the words in which *oo* has the vowel sound in *soon*.

205

LITERATURE
Short Story

Listen to the Audio.
First, listen for the main points. Then listen again for the important details. Take notes as you listen. Retell the story to a partner.

Reading Strategy

Identify Plot and Setting

- The plot is what happens in a story.
- The setting is where a story takes place.
- Picture the plot and the setting in your mind as you read.

Listen as your teacher models the reading strategy.

A Hike Back in Time

by Pam Walker
illustrated by Tom Newsom

Last year, I went to the Grand Canyon for the first time. I wanted to walk the same paths my grandmother walked many years ago and see the same **sights** she saw. As I followed in her **footsteps**, I felt like I was taking a trip back in time!

---

sights   things someone can see, often things that are beautiful or unusual

footsteps   same path that someone took before

I never knew my grandmother, but I have a picture of her. She is standing in front of a **waterfall**.

On our first day, my parents and I **paused** at a ledge. We looked down into the deep canyon. "I wonder if that's the trail to the waterfall," I said.

The desert colors were beautiful. I loved the **shades** of browns, greens, and yellows. I wondered what my grandmother had thought when she looked across the canyon. Had the sun warmed her face the way it warmed mine?

---

waterfall   water that falls down over a cliff

paused   stopped for a short time

shades   darkness and lightness of colors

Before You Go On   In the canyon, the girl thinks of her grandmother. Why?

We walked for a long time along the trail, but we didn't find the waterfall. As the sun rose higher in the sky, we put on hats to **shade** our faces.

My dad said, "Maybe we should turn back and get a **fresh** start tomorrow."

Then I saw a sign. "Supai!" I said. "That's the village I read about. Maybe somebody there knows about the waterfall."

"What do you think?" my dad asked my mom.

"Well, we've come this far," Mom said. "I think we should keep going."

"On to Supai!" I cried.

---

shade protect from direct light

fresh new

In Supai, we met an old man who worked at a store. I asked if I could take his picture for my **scrapbook**.

Then I showed him the picture of my grandmother. He smiled when he looked at the picture and said that my grandmother had a kind face.

"I want to find the same waterfall," I informed him. "I want to see all the things my grandmother saw."

"That's Mooney Falls," he said. "Stay at the **lodge** tonight and go there in the morning."

"Can we, Dad?" I asked. "Can we, Mom?"

"Well, we've come this far," they said.

---

scrapbook   book to store or other things you want to keep

lodge   hotel often in the country

Before You Go On   Why does the girl want to go to Mooney Falls?

I was so excited about hiking to Mooney Falls, I was afraid I wouldn't sleep. But I did sleep because our long hike had made me tired. I fell asleep right away.

When I opened my eyes the next morning, my dad was already awake.

"Let's go!" he said. "We have an **appointment** with Mooney Falls, remember?"

"Not so fast," said Mom. "First, we need to get some supplies."

We returned to the store and bought some water, a compass, and a trail map.

"Ready, Mom?" I asked **impatiently**.

"Ready," she said. "Now we're prepared for a long day on the trails."

---

appointment   meeting at a certain time and place

impatiently   not wanting to wait

"Hold on to the **chain**!" Mom said.

"Watch your step!" Dad said.

We hiked deeper and deeper into the canyon. Each trail was more thrilling than the last.

"I'm glad we bought the trail map," I said. "Supai seems so far away."

Mom smiled. "I know how much you want to find Mooney Falls," she said. "I want to find it, too."

"Do you think Grandmother used a trail map?" I asked.

"No," Mom said. "My mother knew this canyon. It was like her own backyard. She could thrive in the **wilderness**."

"Shhh," Dad said. "I hear something."

---

chain   metal rings connected together in a line

wilderness   large land area that humans have not changed

Before You Go On   How were they **equipped** for the long hike?

We heard the **faint** sound of water in the distance. As we walked, the noise got louder and the air felt cooler. Then we turned a corner, and the trail stopped. I saw a tall waterfall pouring into a clear pool.

"Mooney Falls!" I cried.

I **glanced** at my grandmother's picture. "It looks just like it did fifty years ago."

I dipped my hand into the cool water and let it pour through my fingers. I wondered if my grandmother had done the same thing.

"We should go back," Dad said. "But first, we need a picture."

---

faint   hard to hear

glanced   quickly looked at

I stood in front of the waterfall while Dad pulled
the camera out of his bag.

"Wait a **second**," Mom said. She picked up a stick
from the side of the trail. "You need a walking stick.
Now, you look just like your grandmother."

I looked at the picture again and then held it up.
"Grandmother and I are visiting the waterfall together!"

---

second   very short period of time

206–208

Reading Strategy

Identify Plot and Setting

- What is the plot of this story?

- What is the setting of this story?

- Did thinking about the plot and setting help you understand this story? How?

Think It Over

1. **Recall**   Where are the characters going?

2. **Comprehend**   What **route** do the characters take to the waterfall?

3. **Analyze**   Why is the narrator **motivated** to go on this hike and find the waterfall?

Learning Strategies

Plot and Setting

The **plot** is what happens in a story or play.
The **setting** is the place, date, and time when
the plot happens.

- As you read, look for details that tell you where
and when the events happen.

Practice

**Read the paragraph. Answer the questions about
the plot and setting.**

Last year, I went to the Grand Canyon for the first time.
I walked the same paths my grandmother walked many
years ago. I saw the same sights she saw. As I followed in
her footsteps, I felt like I was taking a trip back in time!

PLOT	SETTING
1. What happens first?	4. Where does this scene occur?
2. What happens next?	5. When does this scene occur?
3. What happens last?	

Use a Sequence of Events Chart

A Sequence of Events Chart can help you record the main events of a story's plot.

 **Practice** G.O. 144

Copy this chart. Write the major events that occur in *A Hike Back in Time.* Then write about the setting of each event.

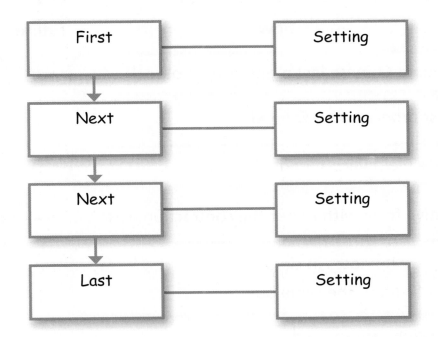

 W B 209

 **Apply**

Reread the story and take notes.
Retell the story to a partner.

Extension

Utilize Would the plot of the story change if the setting were different? Choose a new setting. Draw the scene. List plot changes. Present your new story to the class.

Grammar

Past Progressive

The **past progressive** is used to show an ongoing action that occurred at a specific time in the past.

action

←————————————————————————————————————→

past   **now**   **future**

> I **was studying** Chinese **last night** at nine o'clock.

Here is how past progressive is formed.

> was, were + plain verb + -*ing*

Make the negative form with *not* or the contraction *wasn't* or *weren't*.

> I **was not passing** notes in class.
>
> They **weren't riding** the same bus.

Notice how questions are formed.

> Where **were** you **going** Saturday morning?
>
> Why **was** he **studying** after school?

The past progressive with the simple past shows an ongoing action that is interrupted by another action. It often appears with *when* and *while*.

> While we **were studying,** the doorbell **rang**.
>
> When I **was taking** a walk, it started to **rain**.

Practice

Change each simple past verb to the past progressive tense. Write the sentences.

Example: (hike) The family _____ the trails last night.

The family <u>was hiking</u> the trails last night.

1. (visit) They _____ Italy last summer during the heat wave.

2. (hike) Some people _____ while others built a fire.

3. (play) Tom _____ video games after dinner.

4. (use) We _____ the same book last week.

5. (ride) Who _____ the mules down the canyon ?

Apply

Work with a partner. Take turns telling your partner what you were doing at these times.

Example: A: What were you doing on Saturday at ten o'clock in the morning?

B: I was watching television.

210

- Saturday at ten o'clock in the morning

- Monday at five o'clock in the afternoon

- Tuesday at nine o'clock in the morning

- Friday at midnight

- Sunday at two o'clock in the afternoon

Grammar Check ✔

What kind of actions does the past progressive describe?

Writing

Ongoing Writing Skills Practice

Paraphrasing a Source

When you put an author's ideas into your own words, you are paraphrasing. In this lesson, you will learn how to paraphrase information and ideas from the sources you use in your research.

How to Paraphrase

Follow these steps to paraphrase ideas or information from a source:

1. Read the information in the reference source several times, so the important facts are clear in your mind.

2. Put the source away, and write what you learned in your own words.

3. Look at your source again to make sure all the facts in your paraphrase are correct.

4. Finally, make a note of who wrote the book or article, as well as when it was published and who published it. If the information comes from a website, look for an author's name on the site, or copy down the URL. This information is called a citation.

Task

Begin to research the topic you chose in the last lesson. This will become the research report you will write in the workshop at the end of the unit. To practice paraphrasing, choose a paragraph from one of your sources. Express the ideas in you own words. List the text from the original source, your paraphrase, and the citation in the graphic organizer.

A student named Jamie listed his ideas in this chart:

Text from Source	Paraphrase	Citation
"The holiday was first observed in Philadelphia on July 8, 1776, at which time the Declaration of Independence was read aloud, city bells rang, and bands played."	On July 8, 1776, Philadelphia first observed this holiday. There was a public reading of the Declaration of Independence. Bands played and city bells rang out.	The History of July 4th. History.Com. 23 December 2009 http://www.history.com/content/fourthofjuly/history--of--july--4th

Here is part of Jamie's research report that includes a paraphrase of the information he found on a website. He will use this paraphrase as part of his final research report. He included a description of the source he used for the information.

Jamie Martinez

Imagine you were there at the first Independence Day? What would you see?

On July 8, 1776, Philadelphia first observed this holiday with a public reading of the Declaration of Independence. On this special occasion, bands played and city bells rang out.

Works Consulted List

The History of July 4th. History.Com. 23 December 2009 http://www.history.com/content/fourthofjuly/history--of--july--4th

211–212

What You Will Learn

Reading

- Vocabulary building: *Context, word study*
- Reading strategy: *Summarize*
- Text type: *Informational text (social studies)*

Grammar

Complex sentences: *because, so*

Writing

Quoting a source

These words will help you understand the reading.

Key Words

worth

trade

bartered

currency

rulers

Key Words

The History of Money tells about the history of how trading animals slowly changed into the use of coins and paper money.

Words in Context Audio

1 Cows were worth a lot to people in the past because they provided milk.

2 In the past, people would trade many chickens for one cow.

3 The students in the lunchroom bartered their lunches with each other.

④ Sea shells were a form of currency that people used to buy goods.

⑤ The rulers of countries often have their faces stamped on coins.

Practice

Add a page to your vocabulary notebook.

- Write a sentence but leave a blank where the key word should be.

- Then exchange notebooks with a partner and fill in the missing key words.

Make Connections

Have you ever made a trade to get something you wanted instead of using money? Maybe you have traded work, like washing the dishes?

These words will help you talk about the reading.

cooperate
work together with someone else

initial
happening at the beginning

tradition
something that people have done for a long time and continue to do

Academic Words

Words in Context

Some of the players refused to **cooperate** with the rest of the team.

The **initial** step is to write down your ideas. Then you can start to write your first draft.

This country has a long **tradition** of welcoming new people.

Practice

Write the sentences in your notebook. Choose an academic word to complete each sentence.

1. Many families have at least one _____ that they pass down from parent to child.

2. His _____ report didn't have enough details, but then he added more.

3. Everyone wanted to _____ so that the project would be done well.

Apply

Ask and answer with a partner.

1. Why should you **cooperate** with your classmates?

2. What was your **initial** response to the first day of school?

3. What is your favorite family **tradition**?

Word Study

Greek and Latin Roots

Many English words come from Greek or Latin. For example, the word *annual* means *yearly.* It comes from the Latin root, *anno*, meaning *year.*

Rule

Look for this pattern in English: words that have Greek and Latin roots within them.

The Greek or Latin root in each word is in red.

location   initial
biologist   aquarium

Reading Skill

Looking for patterns in English will make you a better reader.

Practice

Complete each statement.

1. The root *init* means "beginning." The **initial** class was the _____.

   a. last   b. second   c. first

2. The root *loc* means "place." **Location** is _____ something occurs.

   a. when   b. where   c. why

3. The root *aqua* means "water." In an **aquarium** there are _____.

   a. fish   b. birds   c. mice

4. The root *bio* means "life." A **biologist** studies _____.

   a. rocks   b. stars   c. animals

215

More About

How does the history of money tell us about the past?

Audio Listen to the Audio.

First, listen for the main points. Then listen again for the important details. Take notes as you listen. Retell the selection to a partner.

Reading Strategy

Summarize

To summarize a reading selection, you retell the selection's main ideas and important details in your own words. To help you summarize, ask yourself *Who, What, Where, When,* and *Why* questions as you read.

Listen as your teacher models the reading strategy.

The History of Money

by Mbeke Tsango

What is money? The answer might surprise you. Money is what people agree it is. People agree that a pen is worth a dollar, or that an apple is worth an orange.

Did you ever trade an apple for an orange at lunch? If you did, you used your fruit like money. Before money was made for the first time, people bartered, or traded for things they wanted. They traded one thing for another.

Cows, goats, pigs, and sheep were the first currency. Later, farmers traded the things they grew.

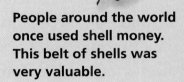

   The first "money" was animals. Then, when people began to farm, they traded vegetables, fruits, and grains. But people wanted money that was easier to carry. That's why early cultures around the world used shells as currency. People agreed on the **value** of each shell. Then they used shells to buy or sell things. In North America, Native Americans and Europeans used shells until the 1800s.

   About 3,000 years ago, people in China began using metals to make shells. Then they made coins. Slowly, metal currency spread to other countries. People made coins from gold, silver, or bronze. The coins were **stamped** with art or images, such as rulers' faces.

People around the world once used shell money. This belt of shells was very valuable.

---

value   the worth or importance of something

stamped   marked or impressed with a design

How are these Asian coins different from American coins?

Before You Go On   Why did people use shells as currency?

Coins of different values have different designs and weights.

At first, people weighed coins to learn their values. Later, each kind of coin got the same size, weight, and decoration.

Paper money was first made in China around 900. People in Europe did not use paper money until about 1650. Soon, paper money became as common as coins.

People still use paper and metal currency. But computers are changing the way we use money. Now we get money from machines. We use plastic **credit cards** to buy things in stores and on the Internet.

Do you think we will use dollars and coins much longer?

Computers are changing the way we use money.

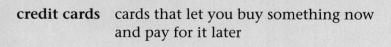

credit cards   cards that let you buy something now and pay for it later

Currency Timeline

9000 B.C.E.	animals
6000 B.C.E.	fruits and vegetables
1200 B.C.E.	shells
1100 B.C.E.	metal coins
900	paper money in Europe
1700	shells in North America
Today	credit cards, debit cards
Future	no bills or coins?

216–218

Reading Strategy

Summarize

- *What* is money?
- *Why* is money important?
- *Where* did people first start making metal "shells" for money?
- *When* were metal coins invented?
- *Whose* faces were stamped on early coins?
- *How* could people **cooperate** with each other instead of using money?

Think It Over!

1. **Recall** What was the **initial** form of money?

2. **Comprehend** Why did people start using shells for money?

3. **Analyze** How do you think it became a **tradition** to stamp rulers' faces on early coins?

Learning Strategies

Summarize

When you **summarize,** you retell the main ideas and details of a story. The main idea and the details are the most important parts of a story.

- Ask yourself **who, what, where, when,** and **why** questions to find the main idea of a story.
- Look for details that support the main idea.

Practice

Reread *The History of Money*. Look at the pictures. Then answer the questions to complete the Details column.

QUESTIONS ABOUT THE MAIN IDEA	DETAILS
1. Who invented metal coins?	1. the Chinese
2. What types of metal were the coins made of?	2.
3. How did people first determine how much a coin was worth?	3.
4. How have computers changed the way we use money?	4.

When the students traded a banana for an apple, they bartered.

Use a Main Idea and Details Chart

A Main Idea and Details Chart helps you record the main idea and the most important details as you read.

Use the chart on the previous page to help you.

- Find the main idea of the selection.
- Then list three details that support that idea.

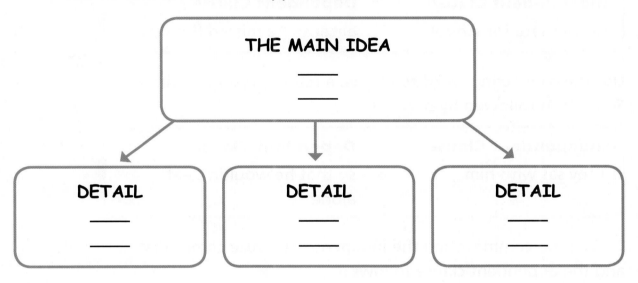

THE MAIN IDEA

____
____

DETAIL

____
____

DETAIL

____
____

DETAIL

____
____

Summarize the story to a partner. Use the key words as you speak.

W B
219

Extension

Utilize Imagine you get to design a special coin to celebrate the year in America. What kinds of things would you include on your coin? Discuss your ideas with a partner. Then present them to the class using pictures.

READING 3 **365**

Grammar

Complex Sentences: *because, so*

A **complex sentence** contains an independent clause (a subject and a verb), a connecting word, and a dependent clause. We use the connecting word *because* to give a reason.

Independent Clause	Dependent Clause
He was late for school	**because** he missed the bus.

Use the connecting word *so* to give a reason, result, or aim. *So* is often followed by *that*.

Independent Clause	Dependent Clause
They sat with him	**so** that he wouldn't eat alone.

There is no comma when the independent clause comes first and the dependent clause follows it.

The dependent clause can occur at the beginning of the sentence, too. There is a comma when the dependent clause comes first.

Dependent Clause	Independent Clause
Because they missed Alabama,	they moved back.
So we could sit together,	they got extra chairs for us.

Practice

Use connecting words *because* or *so* in these complex sentences.

Example: <u>Because</u> shells were easy to carry, people used them as currency.

1. Apples and oranges are worth the same, _____ they can be traded.

2. Chinese coins were different _____ they had holes in them.

3. _____ they don't have to carry money, many people use credit cards.

4. People study history _____ that they keep their **traditions**.

5. _____ people needed to trade things, money was invented.

Apply

Work with a partner. Answer the questions below about *The History of Money.* Use complex sentences.

Example: A: People traded animals because they needed them to live.

B: People use credit cards so they can buy things without cash.

220

- Why did people switch from using animals and vegetables as money to using shells?
- Why did people put the faces of their rulers on their coins and money?
- Why did people weigh early coins?
- Why do you think the Chinese invented paper money?

Grammar Check ✔

What does a complex sentence consist of?

Writing

Quoting a Source

Including quotations from a source in a research report can be an excellent way of supporting your own ideas. In this lesson you will learn how to use quotations in this way.

How to Include Quotations

Follow these steps to quote information directly from a source:

1. Read the text you would like to quote. Think about why you wish to include it in your report. Does it support an idea in a way that you wouldn't be able to do in your own words?

2. Write down the information word-for-word. It may be a sentence or an entire paragraph.

3. Look at your original source again. Make sure you have copied the words correctly.

4. Finally, make a note of who wrote the book or article, when it was published, and who published it. If the information comes from a website, look for an author's name or copy down the URL. This information is for the citation.

5. When you write your report, surround the quoted text in quotation marks. Include your citation.

Task

Continue the research for your report. To practice including quotations, look for information that supports a key point or idea in your report. Copy the text word-for-word. List the idea you want to support, the quotation, and the citation in a graphic organizer.

A student named Jamie listed his ideas in this chart:

Information Search	Direct Quote	Citation
Looking for information about Independence Day	"This is why July 4, the birthday of the United States, is also called Independence Day."	Landau, Elaine. <u>Independence Day: Birthday of the United States.</u> New Jersey: Enslow Publishers, Inc. 2001, p. 12

Here is a paragraph from Jamie's research report. The paragraph includes a quotation. Jamie included information about the book at the end of his report. He included the author's last name in parenthesis at the end of the quotation in his research report.

Jamie Martinez

Independence Day celebrates the official adoption of the Declaration of Independence by the Continental Congress on July 4, 1776. "This is why July 4, the birthday of the United States, is also called Independence Day." (Landau) On July 8, 1776, Philadelphia first observed this holiday with a public reading of the Declaration of Independence in Independence Square.

Works Consulted List

Landau, Elaine. <u>Independence Day: Birthday of the United States.</u> New Jersey: Enslow Publishers, Inc., 2001, p. 12

Apply and Extend

Link the Readings

Copy the chart into your notebook. Read the words in the top row. Then follow these steps:

- For *The Moon Tree*, put an X under the words that remind you of the text.

- Repeat the same activity for *A Hike Back in Time* and *The History of Money*.

	Informational Text	Literature	Community Working Together	Family Working Together
The Moon Tree				
A Hike Back in Time				
The History of Money				

Discussion

1. In what way do the characters in *The Moon Tree* and *A Hike Back in Time* **achieve** similar goals? Explain.

2. All three readings relate to the idea of **cooperating** with others. Give examples from each reading.

3. How can learning about the history of money teach us how people lived in earlier times?

 What was life like in the past and why should we learn about it?

> **Listening Tip**
>
> If you want to confirm your understanding, you can say, "Do you mean...?"

Projects

Your teacher will help you choose one of these projects.

Written	Oral	Visual/Active
Song	**Oral Report**	**Pantomime**
Write a song about going to the Grand Canyon. Use a tune you like or create a new tune. Write words to tell about the Grand Canyon.	Deliver an oral report to your classmates. Tell what you learned about hiking and going to the Grand Canyon.	Reread one of the stories. Act out a part of one story. Ask classmates to guess which story you are acting out.
History Article	**Tall Tale**	**Park Design**
Choose an individual or event from history. Research and write a short article. Ask and answer the 5W questions in your article.	A tall tale stretches the facts about a person or an event. Make up a tall tale about a person or an event from the past.	Design a historical park. Think about what kinds of buildings and exhibits you would include. Create a map or model for the park.

Further Reading

 For more projects visit
LongmanCornerstone.com

Aladdin and the Lamp

This Penguin Young Reader® is a folktale version of the classic fairytale. It is set in China, a long time ago.

Mr. Lincoln's Whiskers, Karen B. Winnick

This story is based on actual correspondence between Abraham Lincoln and eleven-year-old Grace Bedell. In 1860, Grace suggested that growing a beard could help Mr. Lincoln win the presidential election. He grew a beard—and became our first bearded president.

223–224

Listening and Speaking Workshop

Give an Oral Report

You are going to write and give an oral report. Then you will listen as your classmates give an oral report.

❶ Prepare

A. Think about an historical event that happened in your community, this country, or another country. Then give an oral report about why the event was important.

B. Choose an event and research it. Organize the facts, details, and examples. You will need to describe the event and explain why it is important. Write your main points and details on note cards. Find photos, posters, or other visuals to show during your oral report.

Note Card 1

    Main Point — the *Apollo 11* space mission

    Detail — launched on July 16, 1969

    Detail — astronauts first landed on the moon

Note Card 2

    Main Point — very important for NASA and for the world

    Detail — for NASA, first successful space walk

    Detail — for the world, greatest scientific achievement

---

❷ Practice

Practice your oral presentation with your props. Practice in front of your family or friends. If possible, record your oral presentation. Then listen to yourself. How do you sound? Record yourself again and try to improve.

❸ Present

As you speak, do the following:
- Speak clearly and confidently.
- Look at your audience. Glance at your note cards occasionally.
- Use your props and other visuals.

As you listen, do the following:
- Take notes of important points.
- Watch for gestures and pay attention to visuals. Your teacher will ask you questions about the presentation.

> **Speaking** Skills
>
> An oral presentation is a formal situation. Use complete sentences and vocabulary that suits the occasion and audience.

❹ Evaluate

After you speak, answer these questions:
- ✓ Did you speak clearly and with confidence?
- ✓ Did you support your main points with facts, examples, and details?

After you listen, answer these questions:
- ✓ Did you hear the speaker easily?
- ✓ Did you understand the general meaning, main points, and details? Retell it to a partner.
- ✓ Did you take good notes?

> **Listening** Skills
>
> Listen carefully for clearly stated information. It can be used to infer ideas that aren't stated directly.

Writing Workshop

Write a Research Report

Writing Prompt

Write a research report that you began earlier in this unit. Present a main idea, and include facts and details to support it. Gather information from a variety of sources such as books, magazines, or online websites.

❶ Prewrite

Review the lessons in this unit. You have chosen and narrowed a topic. You have created a research plan. You have learned to paraphrase and quote directly from your sources.

A. Taking Notes

Now it is time to do your research. As you do so, you will take notes on your findings. One of the most important things you need to do as you research is to keep track of your sources.

A good way to do this is to use note cards. Use one note card for each idea. Write a label for the idea at the top of the card. Then write your paraphrase or your quotation in the body of the card. Finally, write the source, author, publisher, and page number at the bottom of the card.

You will use your cards when you plan your outline and write your report. You can also use them to put your sources in alphabetical order for your Works Consulted list.

Here is an example of a note card:

FIRST PUBLIC READING OF THE DECLARATION OF INDEPENDENCE

On July 8, 1776, Philadelphia first observed this holiday.
There was a public reading of the Declaration of Independence.
Bands played and city bells rang out.
Source: "The History of July 4th." History.Com. 23 December 2009
http://www.history.com/content/fourthofjuly/history—of—july—4th

B. Making an Outline

Use the labels on your note cards to sort the cards by ideas. Decide
what order you would like to present the ideas in your report.
Discard any note cards that you decide not to use. Once you are
satisfied with the arrangement of your ideas, create an outline.

The Fourth of July

A. Introduction: How to celebrate the Fourth of July
   1. Family picnics
   2. Watch parades and fireworks

B. History: American colonies want freedom.
   1. Declaration of Independence finished July 4, 1776
   2. American colonies fought for freedom from Great Britain

C. History: Holiday
   1. July 8, 1776 first Independence Day in Philadelphia
   2. July 4, 1777 celebration in Philadelphia with fireworks
      and bonfires
D. Conclusion: 1870 Independence Day becomes a national holiday

❷ Draft

Use your outline to help you write a first draft.

- Begin with a paragraph that clearly presents your topic.
- Use transition words to keep your ideas flowing smoothly.
- Include citations for paraphrases and quotations.

Six Traits of Writing Checklist

✔ **Ideas**
Does my first paragraph present the topic clearly?

✔ **Organization**
Are my ideas presented in a logical order?

✔ **Voice**
Is my tone appropriately formal?

✔ **Word Choice**
Do my words express my meaning clearly?

✔ **Sentence Fluency**
Are the sentence patterns varied?

✔ **Conventions**
Did I capitalize proper nouns correctly?

Citing Sources Use the following examples as models:

Book
Pearson, Anne. Ancient Greece. New York: Dorling Kindersley, 2007.

Magazine Article
Fitzgerald, Terrence. "March of the Caterpillars." Natural History September 2008: 28-33.

Internet Website
"Small but WISE." Science News for Kids 6 January 2010. <http://www.sciencenewsforkids.org/articles/20100106/Feature1.asp>

Encyclopedia Article
Lawson, Wendy. "Antarctica." World Book Encyclopedia. 2010 ed.

❸ Revise

Read your draft. Look for places where the writing needs improvement. Use the Writing Checklist to help you identify problems. Then revise your draft.

Here is how Jamie revised his research report:

Jamie Martinez

Why We Celebrate the Fourth of July

Many of us enjoy celebrating the Fourth of July. We like watching parades, having picnics with our families, and watching fireworks at night. We all have a lot of fun, but do you ever wonder why we celebrate the Fourth of July?

Revised to insert missing word.

It is important to remember that this holiday is also known as "Independence Day." On July 4, 1776, American colonists completed the Declaration of Independence. This important document stated that the thirteen American colonies wanted to be free of great britain. In the Revolutionary War, the American colonies fought Great Britain to gain certain things. freedom

Revised to correct errors in capitalization.

Revised to make meaning clearer.

Independence Day celebrates the official adoption of the Declaration of Independence on July 4, 1776. "This is why July 4, the birthday of the United States, is also called Independence Day." (Landau, p. 12)

On July 8, 1776, Philadelphia first observed this holiday with a public reading of the Declaration of Independence in Independence Square. On this special occasion, bands played and city bells rang. One year later, on July 4, 1776, Philadelphia celebarted Independence Day by ringing bells, lighting bonfires, and setting off fireworks.

Revised to correct spelling error.

After America won the Revolutionary War in 1783 Boston and other cities began celebrating this holiday too. In 1870, the U.S. Congress voted to make Independence Day a national holiday. Now towns and cities all over the country celebrate this special holiday.

Revised to correct error in punctuation.

Revised to make meaning clearer.

WORKS CONSULTED LIST

Hershberg, Theodore. "Independence Day."
    World Book Encyclopedia. 2007 ed.

"History of the Fourth." A Capitol Fourth. 20 December 2009.
    <http://www.pbs.org/capitolfourth/history.html>

Landau, Elaine. Independence Day: Birthday of the United States.
    New Jersey: Enslow Publishers, Inc., 2001.

"The History of July 4th." History.Com. 23 December 2009.
        http://www.history.com/content/fourthofjuly/history
        —of—july—4th

❹ Edit

Check your work for errors. Trade papers with a partner.
Use the Peer Review Checklist to give each other feedback.

❺ Publish

Prepare a clean copy of your final draft. Share
your essay with the class.

WB
225–226

Peer Review Checklist

✔ The main ideas and details are clear.

✔ The writing is interesting.

✔ All the information is related to the topic.

Listen to the sentences. Pay attention to the groups of words. Read aloud.

Audio

1. Hector discovers and saves a tree whose seeds went on a space mission.

2. A young girl visits the Grand Canyon and wonders about her grandmother's feelings when she was there.

3. Learning about the history of money is an interesting way to see how people shopped in the past.

Work in pairs. Take turns reading aloud for one minute. Count the number of words you read.

Last year, I went to the Grand Canyon for the first	11
time. I wanted to walk the same paths my grandmother	21
walked. As I followed in her footsteps, I felt like I	32
was taking a trip back in time!	39
I never knew my grandmother, but I have a picture	49
of her. She is standing in front of a waterfall.	59
On our first day, my parents and I paused at a	70
ledge. We looked down into the deep canyon. "I wonder	80
if that's the trail to the waterfall," I said.	89
The desert colors were beautiful. I loved the shades	98
of browns, greens, and yellows. I wondered what my	107
grandmother had thought when she looked across the	115
canyon. Had the sun warmed her face the way it	125
warmed mine?	127

WB
227–228

Test Preparation

Taking Tests

You will often take tests that help show what you know.
Follow these tips to improve your test-taking skills.

Coaching Corner

Answering Test Items for Revising and Editing

- Revising and Editing Tests often ask you to look for corrections and improvements a writer should make.

- Before you read the written selection, preview the questions and answer choices.

- After reading the whole selection, go back and carefully reread the sentence mentioned in the question. Do you notice any mistakes in grammar or punctuation?

- Read each of the answer choices to yourself to see if one of them sounds better than the sentence in the selection. Choose the answer that does the most to improve the whole sentence.

- Remember that sometimes the sentence will not need any corrections or improvements.

Read the following test sample. Study the tips in the box.

229–230

Read the selection. Look for any corrections and improvements that may be needed, then answer the questions.

(1) The city where I live has three interesting museums. (2) They are the Museum of History the Museum of Archaeology, and the Museum of Art. (3) The Museum of History is the largest of the three. (4) I live close to the Museum of History I go there a lot. (5) My mom is a volunteer at some of the events. (6) She says "if you come to our city, try to visit this museum. (7) I agree. (8) There is something for everyone here.

1 What change, if any, should be made in sentence 2?

   A Delete the comma after **Archaeology**

   B Insert a comma after **History**

   C Change *They are* to **They were**

   D Make no change

2 What change, if any, should be made in sentence 4?

   F I go to the museum of History a lot.

   G I go to the close by Museum of History.

   H I live close to the Museum of History, so I go there a lot.

   J No revision is needed.

3 What is the BEST way to revise sentence 6?

   A She says, "if you come to our city." Try to visit this museum

   B She says "If you come to our city try to visit this museum."

   C She says if you come to our city, try to visit this museum."

   D She says, "If you come to our city, try to visit this museum."

Tips

✓ Think about how to combine clauses using connecting words. What's the best way to combine the clauses in sentence 4?

✓ Read each answer choice to yourself. Remember the rules for punctuating quotations.

Handbook

How to Learn Language

Learning a language involves listening, speaking, reading, and writing. You can use these tips to make the most of your language learning.

LISTENING

1. Listen with a purpose.

2. Listen actively.

3. Take notes.

4. Listen to speakers on the radio, television, and Internet.

SPEAKING

1. Think before you speak.

2. Speak appropriately for your audience.

3. Practice reading aloud to a partner.

4. Practice speaking with friends and family members.

5. Remember, it is okay to make mistakes.

READING

1. Read every day.

2. Use the visuals to help you figure out what words mean.

3. Reread parts that you do not understand.

4. Read many kinds of literature.

5. Ask for help.

WRITING

1. Write something every day.

2. Plan your writing before you begin.

3. Read what you write aloud. Ask yourself whether it make sense.

4. Check for spelling and grammar mistakes.

How to Study

Here are some tips for developing good study habits.

- **Schedule a time for studying.** It is easier to develop good study habits if you set aside the same time every day to study. Once you have a study routine, it will be easier for you to find time to prepare for larger projects or tests.

- **Create a special place for studying.** Find a study area where you are comfortable and where you have everything you need for studying. If possible, choose an area that is away from telephones or television. You can play music if it helps your concentration.

- **Read the directions first.** Make sure you understand what you are supposed to do. Ask a partner or your teacher about anything you do not understand.

- **Preview the reading.** Look at the pictures, illustrations, and captions in the reading. They will help you understand the text.

- **Learn unfamiliar words.** Try to figure out what unfamiliar words mean by finding context clues in the reading. If you still can't figure out the meaning, use a dictionary.

- **Take notes.** Keep notes in a notebook or journal of important things you want to remember from the reading.

- **Ask questions.** Write any questions you have from the reading. Discuss them with a partner or your teacher.

How to Build Vocabulary

Use these ideas to help you remember the meanings of new words.

Keep a Vocabulary Notebook Keep a notebook of vocabulary words and their definitions. Test yourself by covering either the word or the definition.

Make Flashcards On the front of an index card, write a word you want to remember. On the back, write the meaning. Use the cards to review the words with a partner or family member.

Say the Words Aloud Use your new words in sentences. Say the sentences to a partner or a family member.

How to Use a Book

The Title Page The title page states the title, the author, and the publisher.

The Table of Contents The table of contents is at the front of a book. The page on which a chapter begins is next to its name.

The Glossary The glossary is a small dictionary at the back of a book. It will tell you the meaning of a word, and sometimes how to pronounce it. Use the glossary the same way you would a dictionary.

The Index The index is at the back of a book. It lists subjects and names that are in the book, along with page numbers where you can find information.

The Bibliography The bibliography at the back of a book or chapter lets you know the books or sources where an author got information.

How to Use a Dictionary and Thesaurus

The Dictionary

You can find the **spelling**, **pronunciation**, **part of speech**, and **definitions** of words in the dictionary.

Pronunciation   Part of Speech

Definitions

let•ter /let´ər/ noun ① one of the signs that you use to write words: *A, B, and C are the first three letters in the English alphabet.*

② a written message that you put into an envelope and send to someone: *I wrote a letter to my friend in Texas.*

Example Sentence

The Thesaurus

A thesaurus is a specialized dictionary that lists **synonyms**, or words with similar meanings, and **antonyms**, or words with opposite meanings. Words in a thesaurus are arranged alphabetically. You can look up the word just as you would look it up in a dictionary.

Main entry: sad
Part of speech: adjective
Definition: unhappy
Synonyms: bitter, depressed, despairing, down, downcast, gloomy, glum, heartbroken, low, melancholy, morose, pessimistic, sorry, troubled, weeping
Antonyms: cheerful, happy

How to Take Tests

Taking tests is part of going to school. Use these tips to help you answer the kinds of questions you often see on tests.

True-False Questions

- If a statement seems true, make sure it is *all* true.
- The word *not* can change the meaning of a statement.
- Pay attention to words such as *all*, *always*, *never*, *no*, *none*, and *only*. They often make a statement false.
- Words such as *generally*, *much*, *many*, *sometimes*, and *usually* often make a statement true.

Multiple Choice Questions

- Try to answer the question before reading the choices. If your answer is one of the choices, choose it.
- Eliminate answers you know are wrong.
- Don't change your answer unless you know it is wrong.

Matching Questions

- Count each group to see whether any items will be left over.
- Read all the items before you start matching.
- Match the items you know first.

Fill-In-the-Blank Questions or Completions

- Read the question or incomplete sentence carefully.
- Look for clues in the question or sentence that might help you figure out the answer.
- If you are given possible answers, cross each out as you use it.

Short Answers and Essays

- Take a few minutes to organize your thoughts.
- Give only the information that is asked for.
- Answer as clearly as possible.
- Leave time to proofread your response or essay.

How to Read Maps and Diagrams

Informational texts often use maps, diagrams, graphs, and charts. These tools help illustrate and explain the topic.

Maps

Maps show the location of places such as countries, states, and cities. They can also show where mountains, rivers, lakes, and streets are located. A compass rose on the map shows which way is north. A scale shows how miles or kilometers are represented on the map.

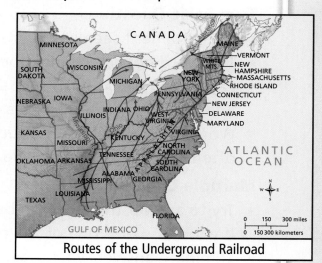

Routes of the Underground Railroad

Diagrams

Diagrams are drawings that explain things or show how things work. Some diagrams show pictures of how objects look on the outside or on the inside. Others show the different steps in a process.

This diagram shows the steps of the Scientific Method. It helps you understand the order and importance of each step.

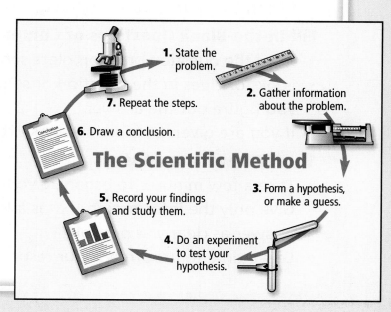

1. State the problem.
2. Gather information about the problem.
3. Form a hypothesis, or make a guess.
4. Do an experiment to test your hypothesis.
5. Record your findings and study them.
6. Draw a conclusion.
7. Repeat the steps.

The Scientific Method

How to Read Graphs

Graphs show how two or more kinds of information are related or alike. Three common kinds of graphs are **line graphs, bar graphs,** and **circle graphs**.

Line Graph

A **line graph** shows how information changes over a period of time. This line graph explains how the Native American population in Central Mexico changed over 100 years.

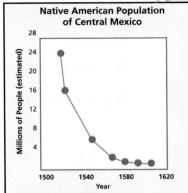

Bar Graphs

We use **bar graphs** to compare information. For example, this bar graph compares the populations of the 13 states in 1790.

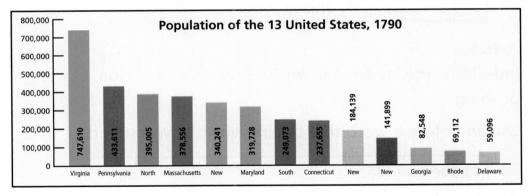

Circle Graphs

A **circle graph** is sometimes called a pie chart because it looks like a pie cut into slices. Circle graphs are used to show how different parts of a whole compare to each other.

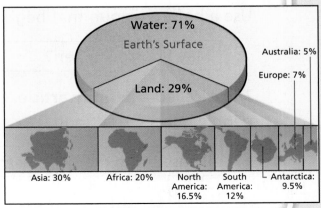

Parts of Speech

In English there are nine **parts of speech**: nouns, articles, pronouns, verbs, adjectives, adverbs, prepositions, conjunctions, and interjections.

Nouns

Nouns name people, places, or things.

A **common noun** is a general person, place, or thing.

> person   thing   place
> The student brings a notebook to class.

A **proper noun** is a specific person, place, or thing.

> person   place   thing
> Joe went to Paris and saw the Eiffel Tower.

Articles

Indefinite articles are *a* or *an*. They refer to a person, place, or thing.

Use *an* before a word that begins with a vowel sound.

> I have an idea.

Use *a* before a noun that begins with a consonant sound.

> May I borrow a pen?

The is called a **definite article**. Use *the* to talk about specific people, places, or things.

> Please bring me the box from your room.

Pronouns

Pronouns are words that take the place of nouns or proper nouns.

proper noun pronoun	
Ana is not home. **She** is babysitting.	

	Subject Pronouns	Object Pronouns
Singular	I, you, he, she, it	me, you, him, her, it
Plural	we, you, they	us, you, them

A **subject pronoun** replaces the subject of a sentence. A **subject** is who or what a sentence is about.

subject   subject pronoun (singular)
Dan is a student. **He** goes to school every day.

Object pronouns replace a noun or proper noun that is the object of a verb. An **object** receives the action of a verb.

object   object pronoun (singular)
Lauren gave **Ed** the notes. Lauren gave **him** the notes.

Possessive pronouns replace nouns or proper nouns. They show who owns something.

	Possessive Pronouns
Singular	mine, yours, hers, his
Plural	ours, yours, theirs

Verbs

Verbs express an action or a state of being.

An **action verb** tells what someone or something does or did.

Verbs that Tell Actions You Can See	Verbs that Tell Actions You Cannot See
dance swim	know sense

A **linking verb** shows no action. It links the subject with another word that describes the subject.

Examples of Linking Verbs		
look	smell	is
are	appear	seem

A helping verb comes before the main verb. They add to a verb's meaning.

	Helping Verbs
Forms of the verb *be*	am, was, is, were, are
Forms of the verb *do*	do, did, does
Forms of the verb *have*	have, had, has
Other helping verbs	can, must, could, have (to), should, may, will, would

Adjectives

Adjectives describe nouns. An adjective usually comes before the noun it describes.

> **tall** grass   **big** truck

An adjective can come *after* the noun it describes. This happens in these kinds of sentences.

> The bag is **heavy**. The books are **new**.

Adverbs

Adverbs describe the action of verbs. They tell *how* an action happens. Adverbs answer the question *Where?, When?, How?, How much?,* or *How often?*

Many adverbs end in *-ly*.

> easily   slowly

Some adverbs do not end in *-ly*.

> seldom   fast   very

In this sentence, the adverb *everywhere* modifies the verb *looked*. It answers the question *Where?*

> verb   adverb
> Nicole looked **everywhere** for her book.

Prepositions

Prepositions show time, place, and direction.

Time	Place	Direction
after	above	across
before	below	down

In this sentence, the preposition *above* shows where the bird flew. It shows place.

> preposition
> A bird flew **above** my head.

In this sentence, the preposition *across* shows direction.

> preposition
> The children walked **across** the street.

A **prepositional phrase** starts with a preposition and ends with a noun or pronoun. In this sentence, the preposition is *near* and the noun is *school*.

> ⌐prepositional phrase⌐
> The library is **near the new school**.

Conjunctions

A **conjunction** joins words, groups of words, and whole sentences. Common conjunctions include *and*, *but*, and *or*.

The conjunction *and* joins two proper nouns: *Allison* and *Teresa*.

> proper   proper
> noun   noun
> Allison **and** Teresa are in school.

The conjunction *or* joins two prepositional phrases: *to the movies* and *to the mall*.

> ⌐prepositional⌐   ⌐prepositional⌐
>   phrase   phrase
> They want to go to the movies **or** to the mall.

The conjunction *but* joins two independent clauses.

> ⌐——independent clause——⌐   ⌐——independent clause——⌐
> Alana baked the cookies, **but** Eric made the lemonade.

Interjections

Interjections are words or phrases that express emotion.

Interjections that express strong emotion are followed by an exclamation point.

> **Wow!** Did you see that catch?

A comma follows interjections that express mild emotion.

> **Gee**, I'm sorry that your team lost.

Sentences

Clauses

Clauses are groups of words with a subject and a verb.

- An **independent clause** can stand on its own as a complete sentence.
- A **dependent clause** cannot stand alone as a complete sentence.

Sentences

A simple sentence is an independent clause. It has a subject and a verb.

> subject   verb
> The dog barked.

A **compound sentence** is made up of two or more simple sentences, or independent clauses.

> ┌──── independent clause ────┐   ┌──── independent clause ────┐
> The band has a lead singer, **but** they need a drummer.

Sentence Types

Declarative sentences are statements. They end with a period.

> We are going to the beach on Saturday.

Interrogative sentences are questions. They end with a question mark.

> Will you come with us?

Imperative sentences are commands. They end with a period or an exclamation point.

> Put on your life jacket. Now jump in the water!

Exclamatory sentences express strong feeling. They end with an exclamation point.

> I swam all the way from the boat to the shore!

Punctuation

End Marks

End marks come at the end of sentences. There are three kinds of end marks: periods, question marks, and exclamation points.

Periods

- Use a period to end a statement (declarative sentence).
- Use a period to end a command or request (imperative sentence).
- Use a period after a person's initial or abbreviated title.
- Use a period after abbreviations.

Question Marks and Exclamation Points

- Use an exclamation point to express strong feelings.
- Use a question mark at the end of a question.

Commas

Commas separate parts of a sentence or phrase.

- Use a comma to separate two independent clauses linked by a conjunction.
- Use commas to separate the parts in a series. A series is a group of three or more words, phrases, or clauses.
- Use a comma to set off introductory words or phrases.
- Use commas to set off an interrupting word or phrase.
- Use a comma to set off a speaker's quoted words.
- Use commas to set off the name of the person being addressed in a letter or speech.

Semicolons and Colons

Semicolons can connect two independent clauses. Use them when the clauses are closely related in meaning or structure.

Colons introduce a list of items or important information. Also use a colon to separate hours and minutes when writing the time.

Quotation Marks

Quotation marks set off direct quotations, dialogue, and some titles.

- Commas and periods always go inside quotation marks.
- If a question mark or exclamation point is not part of the quotation, it goes outside the quotation marks.
- Use quotation marks to set off what people say in a dialogue.
- Use quotation marks around the titles of short works of writing.

Apostrophes

Apostrophes can be used with singular and plural nouns to show ownership or possession. To form the possessive, follow these rules:

- For singular nouns, add an apostrophe and an *s*.
- For singular nouns that end in *s*, add an apostrophe and an *s*.
- For plural nouns that do not end in *s*, add an apostrophe and an *s*.
- For plural nouns that end in *s*, add an apostrophe.
- Apostrophes are also used in contractions, to show where a letter or letters have been taken away.

Capitalization

There are five main reasons to use capital letters:

- to begin a sentence
- to write the pronoun *I*
- to write the names of proper nouns
- to write a person's title
- to write the title of a work (artwork, written work)

Modes of Writing

Narrative Writing is used to tell a story. Here are some types of narrative writing.

- Autobiography is the story of a person's life, told by the person.
- Biography is the story of a person's life told by another person.
- A short story is a short fictional narrative.

Descriptive Writing paints a picture of a person, place, thing, or event.

Expository Writing gives information or explains something. Here are some types of expository writing.

- Compare and Contrast writing analyzes the similarities and differences between two or more things.
- Cause and Effect writing explains why something happened and what happens as a result.
- Problem and Solution writing describes a problem and offers one or more solutions to it.
- How-to writing explains how to do or make something.

Persuasive Writing is writing that tries to convince people to think or act in a certain way.

Functional Writing is writing for real-world uses. Here are some types of functional writing.

- You might fill out a form to sign up for lessons, take a field trip, or apply for a library card.
- You might create an invitation to a holiday party.

The Writing Process

The writing process is a series of steps that helps you write clearly.

Step 1: Prewrite
When you pre-write, you explore ideas and choose a topic. You identify your audience, and you choose your purpose for writing.

To choose a topic, try one or more of these strategies.
- **List** many ideas that you might want to write about.
- **Freewrite** about some ideas for five minutes.
- **Brainstorm** a list of ideas with a partner.

To identify your audience, think about who will read your writing. What do they already know? What do you need to explain?

To identify your purpose for writing, ask:
- Do I want to entertain my audience?
- Do I want to inform my audience?
- Do I want to persuade my audience?

Now, decide on the best form for your writing. Gather and organize the details that will support your topic.

Step 2: Draft
You start writing in this step. Put your ideas into sentences. Put your sentences into paragraphs. Begin to put your paragraphs in order. Don't worry too much about grammar and spelling. You will have a chance to correct any errors later.

Step 3: Revise

This is the time to look at your ideas and the organization of your writing. Read your first draft. Ask yourself:

- Are the ideas presented in the best order?
- Is there a clear beginning, middle, and end?
- Does each paragraph have a main idea and supporting details?

Decide what changes you will make. Then revise your draft.

Step 4: Edit/Proofread

This is the time to look at word choice, sentence fluency, and writing conventions. Reread your paper. Proofread for mistakes in spelling, grammar, and punctuation. Correct any mistakes you find.

When you edit and proofread your draft, use these proofreading marks to mark the changes.

Editing/Proofreading Marks		
To:	**Use This Mark:**	**Example:**
add something	∧	We ate rice, bean**s** and corn.
delete something	ℒ	We ate rice, beans, and corn**s.**
start a new paragraph	¶	¶ We ate rice, beans, and corn.
add a comma	﹂	We ate rice, beans and corn.
add a period	⊙	We ate rice, beans, and corn⊙
switch letters or words	∼	We ate rice, baens, and corn.
change to a capital letter	<u>a</u>	we ate rice, beans, and corn.
change to a lowercase letter	⁄A	WE ate rice, beans, and corn.

Peer Review Checklist

Ideas

☐ Is the content interesting and thoughtful?
☐ Is the main idea clearly stated?
☐ Are the main ideas supported by facts and details?
☐ Do the ideas flow from one to the next?

Organization

☐ Are the ideas in an order that makes sense?
☐ Are the ideas connected by transitions and other connecting words?

Voice

☐ Does the writing have energy and personality?

Word Choice

☐ Has the writer chosen precise words?

Sentence Fluency

☐ Do the sentences flow smoothly?
☐ Are the sentences varied in type and length?

Conventions

☐ Do the subjects of sentences agree with the verbs?
☐ Do the pronouns agree with the words they refer to?
☐ Are the verb tenses appropriate and consistent?
☐ Is the possessive case (apostrophe -s) used correctly?
☐ Are negatives and contractions used correctly?
☐ Are the punctuation and capitalization correct?
☐ Is the writing free of spelling errors?

Step 5: Publish

Once you have revised and proofread your paper, share it with others. Look at these publishing ideas.

- Post your paper on the bulletin board.
- Photocopy your paper. Hand it out to your classmates and family members.
- Attach it to an email and send it to friends.
- Sent it to a school newspaper or magazine for possible publication.

Once you have shared your work with others, you may want to put it in your portfolio. A portfolio is a folder or envelope in which you keep your writing. If you keep your work in a portfolio, you can look at what you have written over a period of time. This will let you see if your writing is improving. It will help you become a better writer.

Build Your Portfolio

You may want to keep your completed writing in your portfolio. It is a good idea to keep your drafts, too. Keep comments you receive from your teacher or writing partner, as well.

Reflect on Your Writing

Make notes on your writing in a journal. Write how you felt about what you wrote. Use these questions to help you get started.

- What new things did you learn about your topic?
- What helped you organize the details in your writing?
- What helped you revise your writing?
- What did you learn about yourself as you wrote?

Rubric for Writing

A rubric is a tool that helps you assess, or evaluate, your work. This rubric shows specific details for you to think about when you write. The scale ranges from 4 to 1, with 4 being the highest score and 1 being the lowest.

4	Writing is clearly focused on the task. Writing is well organized. Ideas follow a logical order. Main idea is fully developed and supported with details. Sentence structure is varied. Writing is free of fragments. There are no errors in writing conventions.
3	Writing is focused, with some unnecessary information. There is clear organization, with some ideas out of order. The main idea is supported, but development is uneven. Sentence structure is mostly varied, with some fragments. Writing conventions are generally followed.
2	Writing is related to the task but lacks focus. Organization is not clear. Ideas do not fit well together. There is little or no support for the main idea. No variation in sentence structure. Fragments occur often. Frequent errors in writing conventions.
1	The writing is generally unfocused. There is little organization or development. There is no clear main idea. Sentence structure is unvaried. There are many fragments. Many errors in writing conventions and spelling.

Writing and Research

Sometimes when you write, you need to do research to learn more information about your topic. You can do research in the library, on the Internet, and by viewing or listening to information media.

Library Reference

Encyclopedias contain basic facts, background information, and suggestions for additional research.

Biographical references provide brief life histories of famous people in many different fields.

Almanacs contain facts and statistics about many subjects, including government, world history, geography, entertainment, business, and sports.

Periodicals are past editions of magazines. Use a periodical index to find articles on your topic.

Vertical files contain pamphlets on a wide variety of topics.

Electronic databases provide quick access to information on many topics.

Citing Sources

When you do research, you read what other people wrote. The material you research is called the source or reference. When you tell who wrote the material, this is called citing the source. It is important to cite each source you use when you write.

In your paper, note each place in which you use a source. At the end of the paper, provide a list that gives details about all your sources. A bibliography and a works cited list are two types of source lists.

- A **bibliography** provides a listing of all the material you used during your research.

- A **works cited list** shows the sources you have quoted in your paper.

Plagiarism
Plagiarism is presenting someone else's words, ideas, or work as your own. If the idea or words are not yours, be sure to give credit by citing the source in your work. It is a serious offense to plagiarize.

Look at the chart of the Modern Language Association (MLA). Use this format for citing sources. This is the most common format for papers written by middle and high school students, as well as college students.

MLA Style for Listing Sources

Book	Pyles, Thomas. *The Origins and Development of the English Language*. 2nd ed. New York: Harcourt Brace Jovanovich, Inc., 1971.
Signed article in a magazine	Gustaitis, Joseph. "The Sticky History of Chewing Gum." *American History* Oct. 1998: 30–38.
Filmstrips, slide programs, videocassettes, DVDs	*The Diary of Anne Frank*. Dir. George Stevens. Perf. Millie Perkins, Shelly Winters, Joseph Schildkraut, Lou Jacobi, and Richard Beymer. Twentieth Century Fox, 1959.
Internet	*National Association of Chewing Gum Manufacturers*. 19 Dec. 1999. <http://www.nacgm.org/consumer/funfacts.html> [Indicate the date you found the information.]
Newspaper	Thurow, Roger. "South Africans Who Fought for Sanctions Now Scrap for Investors." *Wall Street Journal* 11 Feb. 2000.
Personal interview	Smith, Jane. Personal interview. 10 Feb. 2000.

Internet Research

The Internet is an international network of computers. The World Wide Web is a part of the Internet that lets you find and read information.

To do research on the Internet, you need to open a search engine. Type in a keyword on the search engine page. **Keywords** are words or phrases on the topic you want to learn about. For example, if you are looking for information about your favorite musical group, you might use the band's name as a keyword.

To choose a keyword, write a list of all the words you are considering. Then choose a few of the most important words.

Tips

- Spell the keywords correctly.
- Use the most important keyword first, followed by the less important ones.
- Open the pages at the top of the list first. These will usually be the most useful sources.

 How to Evaluate Information from the Internet

When you do research on the Internet, you need to be sure the information is correct. Use the checklist to decide if you can trust the information on a Web site.

✓ Look at the address bar. A URL that ends in "edu" is connected to a school or university. A URL that ends in "gov" means it is a site posted by a state or federal government. These sites should have correct information.

✓ Check that the people who write or are quoted on the site are experts, not just people telling their ideas or opinions.

✓ Check that the site is free of grammatical and spelling errors. This is often a hint that the site was carefully designed and researched.

✓ Check that the site is not trying to sell a product or persuade people.

✓ If you are not sure about using a site as a source, ask an adult.

Information Media

Media is all the organizations that provide news and information for the public. Media includes television, radio, and newspapers. This chart describes several forms of information media.

Types of Information Media	
Television News Program	• Covers current news events • Gives information objectively
Documentary	• Focuses on one topic of social interest • Sometimes expresses controversial opinions
Television Newsmagazine	• Covers a variety of topics • Entertains and informs
Radio Talk Show	• Covers some current events • Offers a place for people to express opinions
Newspaper Article	• Covers one current event • Gives details and background about the event
Commercial	• Presents products, people, or ideas • Persuades people to buy or take action

How to Evaluate Information from Various Media

Because the media presents large amounts of information, it is important to learn how to analyze this information. Some media sources try to make you think a certain way instead of giving you all the facts. Use these techniques to figure out whether you can trust information from the media.

✓ Sort facts from opinions. A fact is a statement that can be proven true. An opinion is how someone feels or thinks about something. Make sure any opinions are supported by facts.

✓ Be aware of the kind of media you are watching, reading, or listening to. Is it news or a documentary? Is it a commercial? What is its purpose?

✓ Watch out for bias. **Bias** is when the source gives information from only one point of view. Try to gather information from several points of view.

✓ Discuss what you learn from different media with your classmates or teachers. This will help you determine if you can trust the information.

✓ Read the entire article or watch the whole program before reaching a conclusion. Then, develop your own views on the issues, people, and information presented.

How To Use Technology in Writing

Writing on a Computer

You can write using a word processing program. This will help you when you follow the steps in the Writing Process.

- When you write your first draft, save it as a document.
- As you type or revise, you can move words and sentences using the cut, copy, and paste commands.
- When you proofread, you can use the grammar and spell check functions to help you check your work.

Keeping a Portfolio

Create folders to save your writing in. For example, a folder labeled "Writing Projects—September" can contain all of the writing you do during that month.

Save all the drafts of each paper you write.

Computer Tips

- Rename each of your revised drafts using the SAVE AS function. For example, if your first draft is "Cats," name the second draft "Cats2."
- If you share your computer, create a folder for only your work.
- Always back up your portfolio on a server or a CD.

Glossary

A

achieve succeed in doing something (p. 322)

adapt change to fit a new situation (p. 262)

advice a suggestion about what someone should do (p. 216)

affect produce a change in someone or something (p. 204)

anticipate guess or expect that something will happen (p. 172)

appreciate be grateful for something (p. 154)

appropriate fitting; suitable (p. 92)

architects people whose job is to plan and design buildings (p. 230)

architecture shape and style of buildings (p. 260)

ash gray powder that is left after something has been burned (p. 74)

assistance help or support (p. 106)

astronaut someone who travels in space (p. 320)

B

banned officially said that people must not do something or that something is not allowed (p. 44)

bare empty (p. 152)

bartered exchanged one thing for another (p. 356)

bean a seed or seed container of a plant that you eat (p. 202)

benefit something that helps you or gives you an advantage (p. 154)

boasted bragged (p. 170)

bolt white line that appears in the sky (p. 104)

bond special relationship or connection (p. 30)

breath air that you let in and out through your nose and mouth (p. 28)

breeders someone who keeps animals in order to produce babies (p. 44)

breeze light wind (p. 104)

C

canyon deep valley with very steep sides (p. 338)

captured caught (p. 44)

413

celebration an occasion or party when you do something special because of a particular event (p. 202)

challenge something that is hard to do (p. 10)

chapel a small church, or part of a church (p. 290)

climate the weather that a place usually has (p. 274)

communicates exchanges information with others (p. 8)

communities areas in which people live (p. 230)

community group of people who live in the same area (p. 322)

companion someone you are with, often a friend (p. 28)

concerned worried (p. 230)

considerable large enough to be important (p. 292)

consist of made up of (p. 76)

cooperate work together with someone else (p. 358)

correspond write and receive messages with someone (p. 276)

council group of people who are chosen to make laws and decisions (p. 136)

currency money (p. 356)

crater round open top of a volcano (p. 74)

demonstrate show how to do something (p. 92)

display show (p. 172)

duty something you must do because it is right or part of your job (p. 136)

efficient working well, quickly, and without waste (p. 260)

electricity kind of energy (p. 90)

eliminate get rid of something completely (p. 204)

emerge appear or come out from somewhere (p. 138)

encounter a meeting (p. 30)

environment world of land, sea, and air that you live in; your surroundings (p. 262)

equipped provided with things that are needed to do something (p. 340)

erupts explodes and sends out fire and smoke (p. 74)

establish get something started, such as a company, system, or situation, etc. (p. 46)

evaluate judge how good something is (p. 218)

evaporate when a liquid turns into a gas (p. 90)

evidence proof (p. 76)

explorer someone who travels into an unknown area to find out about it (p. 320)

extreme very great (p. 260)

feature a part that stands out (p. 92)

feral domestic animals that now live in the wild (p. 44)

fine very nice or of high quality (p. 152)

flatter say nice things to someone because you are trying to please him or her (p. 216)

frisky full of energy, happiness, and fun (p. 28)

gardener a person who works in a garden (p. 202)

glowed shined with a steady light (p. 28)

goal something you want to achieve (p. 10)

guzzled drank a lot of something eagerly and quickly (p. 216)

harsh very unpleasant, cruel (p. 274)

hiking taking a long walk in the country or in the mountains (p. 338)

homestead a farm and the area of land and buildings around it (p. 290)

hurricane storm with very strong fast winds (p. 104)

impact a strong effect (p. 106)

infer form an opinion that something is probably true because of information that you have (p. 152)

initial happening at the beginning (p. 358)

involve include, or be part of (p. 10)

415

L

labor hard work (p. 292)

lava very hot liquid rock that comes out of the top of a mountain (p. 74)

ledge narrow flat surface of rock that is high above the ground (p. 338)

lightning bright flash of light in the sky that happens during a storm (p. 90)

located be in a particular place (p. 262)

M

machine something mechanical that helps people do work (p. 170)

major big; very important or serious (p. 106)

mighty very strong (p. 170)

mining digging in the ground for coal, iron, gold, etc. (p. 260)

mischief bad behavior, especially by children (p. 136)

mission important job that someone has been given to do (p. 320)

motivated very eager to do or achieve something (p. 340)

mustangs small wild horses (p. 44)

N

native growing or living in a particular place (p. 260)

nonsense ideas or behaviors that are not true or seem stupid or annoying (p. 136)

O

objective goal (p. 232)

occur to happen or take place (p. 30)

orchard a place where fruit trees are grown (p. 290)

original first, earliest (p. 230)

outcome the final result of a meeting, process, etc. (p. 204)

P

pioneer someone who goes somewhere or does something before other people (p. 290)

plaque piece of flat metal or stone with writing on it (p. 320)

prairie large open area of land that is covered in wheat or long grass (p. 274)

praise words that you say to tell someone that he or she has done something well (p. 216)

preserve keep something from being destroyed or changed too much (p. 230)

previously before (p. 276)

protect prevent someone or something from being harmed or damaged (p. 8)

purpose a reason for doing something; aim (p. 230)

react say or do something because of something else (p. 138)

record information that is written down so you can look at it later (p. 274)

recover get better to a healthy condition (p. 46)

reside live somewhere (p. 276)

resourceful good at finding ways to deal with problems effectively (p. 218)

respond answer (p. 138)

restore repair something to make it seem new again (p. 232)

roots parts of a plant that grow under the ground (p. 202)

route the way from one place to another, especially on a map (p. 340)

rulers people who govern a country, such as presidents or kings (p. 356)

satisfied pleased because something has happened in the way that you want (p. 136)

scampered ran with short, quick steps, like a small animal (p. 216)

scenario setting or situation (p. 172)

scheme tricky plan (p. 218)

secure safe (p. 8)

settler someone who goes to live in a new place, usually where there were few people before (p. 290)

shelter a place that protects you from bad weather (p. 104)

shimmer shine with a soft light that seems to shake slightly (p. 28)

signatures people's names, written in their own handwriting (p. 320)

similar almost the same, but not exactly (p. 76)

site place (p. 232)

sledgehammer an extra large and heavy hammer (p. 170)

sod piece of dirt with grass growing on top (p. 274)

sputter make a coughing noise as if breaking down (p. 170)

stitches small lines of thread sewn onto cloth (p. 152)

strategy a plan used to reach a goal (p. 46)

stroke particular moment in time (p. 152)

surrounded to be all around someone or something (p. 320)

temperature how hot or cold something is (p. 90)

thrilling exciting and interesting (p. 338)

thrive be very strong and healthy (p. 338)

thunder loud sound that you hear in the sky during a storm (p. 90)

tidbit small piece of food or information (p. 136)

trade exchange one thing for another (p. 356)

tradition something people have done for a long time and continue to (p. 358)

trails paths across open country, or through mountains or woods (p. 338)

underground under Earth's surface (p. 260)

undertake take on as a responsibility (p. 292)

unique special, one of a kind (p. 322)

vine a plant with long stems that climb on other plants, buildings, etc. (p. 202)

volcano mountain with a hole at the top from which come burning rock and fire (p. 74)

warm slightly hot, but not too hot (p. 28)

whisk quickly take something or someone somewhere (p. 152)

wink close and open one eye quickly (p. 152)

worth value (p. 356)

young not having lived very long (p. 8)

Index

421

Credits

83 top right, Photo Researchers, Inc.; 84-85 Bettmann/CORBIS; 87 Sites & Photos / Alamy; 89 Shargaljut/Dreamstime; 90 top, Photo Researchers, Inc.; 90 bottom left, Dorling Kindersley; 90 bottom middle, Photo Researchers, Inc.; 90 bottom right, Dorling Kindersley; 91 top, Image Bank/Getty Images; 91 bottom left, Corbis Royalty Free; 91 bottom right, Photodisc/Getty Images; 92 Marinko Tarlac/Shutterstock; 93 Mastefile StockImage Library; 94 Corbis Digital Stock; 95 top, Photo Researchers, Inc.; 95 bottom, Photodisc/Getty Images; 101 Murat Yilmaz-Kemal Eroglu/Shutterstock; 104 top, Pearson Education/PH College; 104 bottom, Stock Market/CORBIS; 105 top, AP Wide World Photos; 105 bottom, Stone Allstock/ Getty Images; 106 Photos.com, a division of Getty Images; 107 Randy Faris/CORBIS; 123 LesPalenik/Shutterstock, 126 Zastol`skiy Victor Leonidovich/Shutterstock.

UNIT 3 130-131 Bill Bachman/Alamy; 133 top left, Pearson Learning Photo Studio; 133 bottom left, PhotoEdit Inc.; 133 top right, The Learning Company Inc.; 133 bottom right, Time Life Pictures/Getty Images; 134 left, © Creatista/Shutterstock; 134 left inset, © Eky Studio/Shutterstock; 134 right, Hulton Archive Photos/Getty Images; 134 right inset, PhotoEdit Inc.; 135 left, Gideon Mendel for The International HIV/AIDS Alliance/CORBIS; 135 left inset, Caroline Penn/CORBIS; 135 right, Bettmann/ CORBIS; 135 right inset, © elavuk81/Fotolia; 136 middle, PhotoEdit Inc.; 136 bottom, Stockbyte/Getty Images; 137 top, PhotoEdit Inc.; 137 middle, © Sudio 1One/Fotolia; 137 bottom, PhotoEdit Inc.; 149 Aimin Tang/ iStockphoto; 151 Andrew Howe/iStockphoto; 152 top, The Image Works; 152 middle, Peter Arnold; 152 bottom, Dorling Kindersley; 153 top, Leonard de Selva/CORBIS; 153 middle, Blue Lantern Studio/CORBIS; 153 bottom, PhotoEdit Inc.; 164 Joe_Potato/iStockphoto; 169 Photos.com, a division of Getty Images; 170 top, © Shutterstock; 170 center, © Marko Vesel/Shutterstock; 170 bottom, © Orientaly/ Shutterstock; 171 top, © Sonya Etchison/ Shutterstock; 171 bottom, © Mikael Damkier/ Shutterstock; 173 wsfurlan/iStockphoto; 185 Photos.com, a division of Getty Images; 189 Slobo Mitic/iStockphoto; 192 mb_fotos/Can Stock Photo.

UNIT 4 196-197 Creatas Images/PunchStock; 196 bottom left, Robert W. Ginn/PhotoEdit Inc.; 199 top left, AP Wide World Photos; 199 bottom left, Stone Allstock/Getty Images; 199 top right, Culver Pictures; 199 bottom right, Dorling Kindersley; 200 left, © Kris Hollingsworth/Shutterstock; 200 left inset, Silver Burdett Ginn; 200 right, Photolibrary. com; 200 right inset, Floresco Productions/ CORBIS; 201 top left, Merrill Education; 201 left inset, Mina Chapman/CORBIS/ PunchStock; 201 top right, PhotoEdit Inc.; 201 right inset, Robert Clay Photography; 202 top, Hedda Gjerpen/iStockphoto; 202 center, Larry Korb/Shutterstock; 202 bottom, Steffen Foerster/iStockphoto; 203 top, liseykina/Shutterstock; 203 bottom, Hal_P/Shutterstock; 204 kristian sekulic/ Shutterstock; 205 Photos.com, a division of Getty Images; 206-207 © Rob Hainer/ Shutterstock; 207 Robert W. Ginn/PhotoEdit Inc.; 208 top, The Granger Collection, NY; 208-209 bottom, © Steve Nudson/Alamy; 209 top, Jupiter Images; 209 bottom, 210 AP/Wide World Photos; 211 Jupiter Images; 213 Gabor Izso/iStockphoto; 215 Dmitry Melnikov/Shutterstock; 216 top, Linda Kloosterhof/iStockphoto; 216 center, Maridav/iStockphoto; 216 bottom, digitalskillet/iStockphoto; 217 top, aspen rock/Shutterstock; 217 bottom, SteveStone/ iStockphoto; 218 Photos.com, a division of Getty Images; 219 Brian Swartz/iStockphoto; 224 left, Fernando Delvalle/iStockphoto; 224 right, fotoVoyager/iStockphoto; 229 Bojan Pavlukovic/iStockphoto; 230 top, Heng Kong Chen/iStockphoto; 230 center, Photos.com, a division of Getty Images; 230 bottom, Photos.com, a division of Getty Images; 231 top, Duncan Walker/iStockphoto; 231 bottom left, Photos.com, a division of Getty